John Lennon

JOHN LENNON In His Life   In His Life   In His Life

In His Life   In His Life   In His Life   In His Life   In His Life

WHITE STAR PUBLISHERS

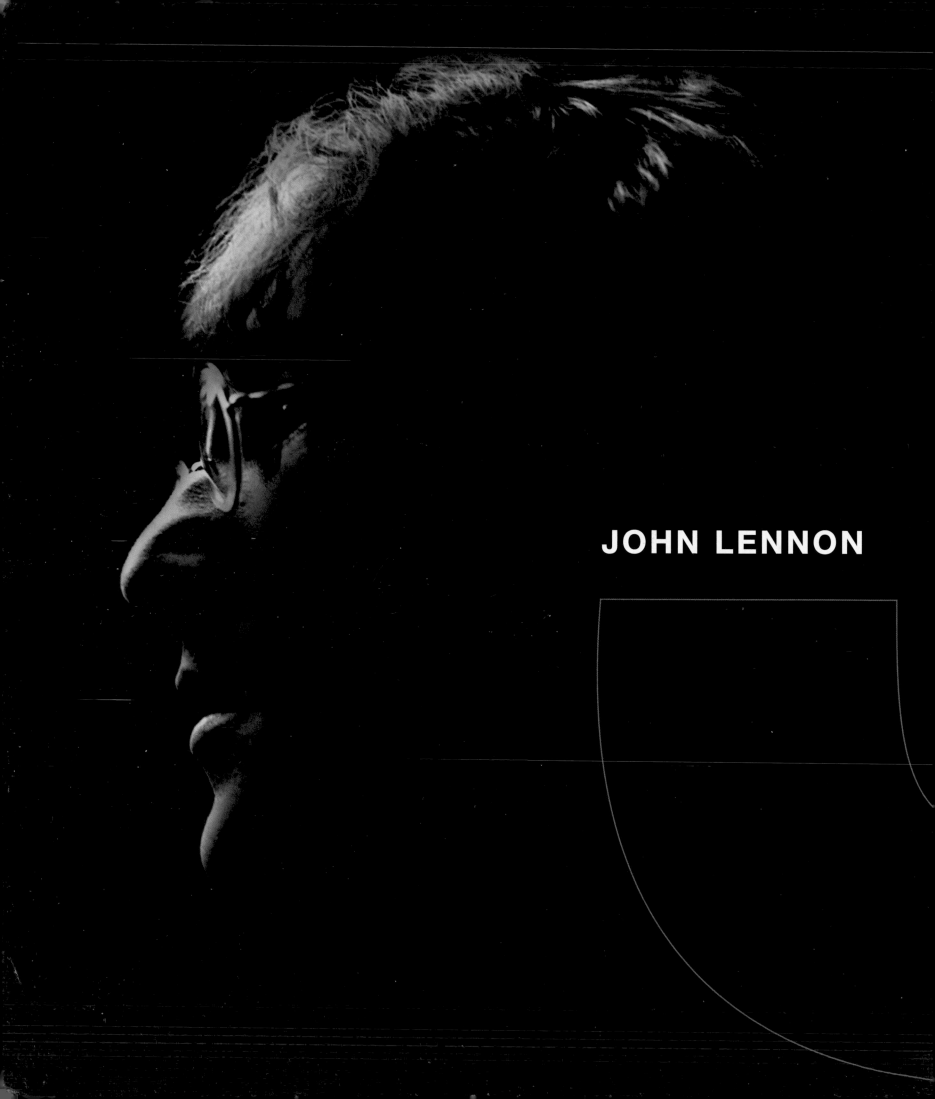

JOHN LENNON

His Life In His Life In His Life In His Life In H s Life In His Life In His Life In His Life

EDITED BY

VALERIA MANFERTO DE FABIANIS

PREFACE

YOKO ONO LENNON

TEXT

JOHN BLANEY

GRAPHIC DESIGN

PATRIZIA BALOCCO LOVISETTI

3 "I was a nice, clean-cut suburban boy." John Lennon

4 "I don't want people taking things from me that aren't really me. They make you something that they want to make you, that isn't really you. We're not The Beatles at all. We're just us." John Lennon

7 John Lennon photographed for the cover of The Beatles' fifth British long-playing record and their second feature-length film, *Help!*

10-11 Lennon had a great awareness about things going on about him. His quick wit and sense of humor gave him the ability to transform difficult situations to his advantage.

13 "If someone thinks that love and peace is a cliché that must have been left behind in the Sixties, that's his problem. Love and peace are eternal." John Lennon

14 When John and Yoko issued their debut album, Paul McCartney's sleeve note was both perceptive and prophetic. "When two great Saints meet it is a humbling experience. The long battles to prove he was a Saint."

19 "My role in society, or any artist's or poet's role, is to try and express what we all feel. Not to tell people how to feel. Not as a preacher, not as a leader, but as a reflection of us all." John Lennon

Contents

LENNON

John Lennon™

The Way We Were

As I looked through the pages of this book, two songs went through my mind, John's masterpiece "In My Life," and the title song from the movie "The Way We Were" by Marvin Hamlisch. That song became "our song" for us, John & Yoko.

John had already lived a very full, whirlwind life when I met him. He was living a dream that most people rarely get to realize. He was making a living at what he did best and loved most, songwriting. But he was always a curious and highly intelligent man and was looking for something more out of life.

When we met in 1966 at my Indica Gallery show little did we know that it was to be the beginning of the new chapter in the life of John and yoko. It was not easy. It was the two of us against the world, but we had each other and held on to each other for dear life.

We were in love with life and each other, planning to one day, sit in our rocking chairs in Cornwall, and wait for our son, Sean's postcards to come to us. That was John's dream. And he told that to me many times. I loved that story because that meant that John was looking forward to us to living a long, long time, in peace. But one day, suddenly, his dream was over.

This book beautifully Illustrates the incredible life of John Lennon. A life which was stranger than fiction, and magical in so many ways.

As John said "Life is what happens to you while you're busy making other plans."

Have fun traveling through his years with him, on every page of this book. You will see that his life illustrated that statement, that while he was dreaming of being in Cornwall, one day, his life went through the changes nobody could have imagined for him.

When I see him in these many different photos, my eyes automatically go to his eyes. You see that sometimes he is keeping his chin up in a very trying situation. But his eyes never lost the sparkle... which kept him going. Enjoy!

Love, Yoko '09

INTRODUCTION

JOHN LENNON IN HIS LIFE

Photographs from Lennon's childhood show a confident, happy, normal young boy. Whether playing with a puppy, posing with a new bicycle or laughing with his mother, they could come from any family album. Lennon, however, was anything but normal. He knew it, his Aunt Mimi knew it and his teachers knew it. But none of them could have known how special he was going to be.

As Paul McCartney would later note, being born in Liverpool carries with it certain responsibilities. If anyone was burdened with such a responsibility it was Lennon. Long before he became the city's greatest son, Liverpool had a deep and lasting affect on him. Like other cities around the world, Liverpool suffered from an inferiority complex. The long established north/south divide, marked it as somehow inferior to London. It was, nevertheless, a vibrant city. Being a port, it enjoyed a cosmopolitan mix of people from around the world. Hard working and vociferous, they developed a unique sense of humor to see them through the harsh realities of everyday life. (Liverpool has probably produced more great comedians than any other British city). Without its rich musical heritage there would have been no Beatles, no "golden era" of pop music and little chance of the 1960s ever swinging. Lennon owed Liverpool a lot, but he gave a lot and helped cement the city's reputation for tolerance, wit and creativity.

Brought up by his aunt and uncle, his early childhood was one of comfortable middleclass conformity – a characteristic he constantly rebelled against. Both his father and grandfather were working class, something he never forgot and strongly identified with. Despite his comfortable middle class childhood, Lennon always sided with the oppressed, regardless of class, color or creed. In his own way he was classless, a real man of the people, a natural leader and indefatigably himself.

Although he was a bright child, he didn't do well at school. He found it uninteresting and continually challenged his teachers' authority. Considering himself more intelligent than them, he didn't suffer fools gladly.

t was a trait that never left him. The things that did interest him: writing, music and art, weren't considered priorities in Britain's post-war education system. Rather than concentrate on his school work, Lennon would spend hours in his bedroom listening to the radio, letting his imagination run free. He loved the BBC radio program, "The Goon Show" and the surreal world it created. He took it as evidence that the world was insane, and yet its own internal logic made perfect sense. Lennon's particular world view dovetailed with the show's main scriptwriter, Spike Milligan, and his writings and drawings bear witness to the show's influence. His cutting humor and insightful intelligence gave him and The Beatles an edge that others could never hope to emulate.

The contradictions Lennon experienced: a real and surrogate mother, poverty and affluence, conformity and rebellion, hardship and prosperity, made him what he was – an artist. Lennon saw the world differently from others, which wasn't always an advantage. Besides getting him into trouble at school, the knowledge that he was different from everybody else caused him a great deal of self-doubt. This wasn't helped by the fact that his parents had abandoned him almost from birth, and that his aunt, who loved him dearly, clearly wanted him to conform. Despite his doubts, Lennon believed from an early age that he was destined for greatness. Call it daydreaming or an early manifestation of his belief in personal projection, but Lennon frequently expected to see his name in reviews, even though he'd yet to write a song or book. Lennon had few toys as a child, but thanks to his aunt and uncle he developed a love of books. His uncle taught him to read from newspapers, a habit that stayed with him. He often drew inspiration from newspapers for his songs, "A Day In The Life" being his best known example. When he wasn't reading, he was writing his own comics, *The Daily Howl,* for the amusement of his friends. His attention span was, however, short, and although he published two books they were little more than collections of ideas jotted down before his butterfly mind moved on to something new. Throughout his career, he liked to work quickly and often became frustrated when technical problems or other interruptions got in his way.

Although Lennon lived apart from his mother, he was brought up in a loving family environment. His aunt doted on him, as did the other women in his life. Summer holidays were spent with his Aunt Mimi in Durness, Scotland – Lennon always retained fond memories of this part of the country. Julia, his mother, visited her sister almost daily, and as Lennon grew older they became very close. They shared similar interests in music and clothes and both had an unorthodox outlook. Julia encouraged his interest in music, something his aunt discouraged. She gave him the confidence to express himself in other ways, too. Under her motherly eye he began to dress in the latest Teddy Boy style. Teddy Boys were the first British subculture to dress purely for style and personal expression. Lennon was beginning to stand out from the crowd rather than blend in as his aunt would have liked

Julia was the centre of Lennon's world; she was more than a mother to him, she was a friend. Paul McCartney spent a lot of time with Lennon and his mother and remembers the way he reacted when he had to leave her and return to his aunt's house. "When we left there was always a tinge of sadness about John. On the way back I could always tell that he loved the visit and loved her but was very sad that he didn't live with her. He loved his Aunt Mimi, I know he did, but she was always the surrogate." Julia's sudden and unexpected death in a road-traffic accident was a tragedy from which Lennon never recovered. He was never the same after his mother's death. It was like somebody had pulled the rug out from under him. Speaking in 1980, he said: "I lost her twice. Once as a five-year-old when I moved in with my auntie. And once again at 17 when she actually physically died... That was a really hard time for me. It just absolutely made me very bitter. The underlying chip on my shoulder as a youth got really big then."

Lennon repressed his pain deep within him, and began building a hard and rugged persona to disguise his anger and low self esteem. Occasionally, it would boil over into violence, but more often than not, Lennon masked it with alcohol and drugs. But once he became a songwriter, he exorcised his demons in the most direct way he could. Unlike his song writing partner, Paul McCartney, Lennon revealed his inner most feelings in a very candid way. Where McCartney would write to disguise the fact that he was often writing about himself, Lennon was painfully honest and open. It was through his song writing that Lennon showed his true colors. His first wife, Cynthia, recalled, "John had this image of being the toughest boy in college but his music showed what all of us knew was underneath. He had a gentleness that needed to come out, and it did in those songs." Eleven years after his mother died, he wrote the beautiful ballad "Julia" for her that showed just how tender he could be.

Music began to play an increasingly important part in his life. Lonnie Donegan and Elvis Presley became his life blood. Astrid Kirchherr, who befriended The Beatles when they were in Hamburg, recalls: "He was obsessed with rock 'n' roll and used to listen to artists like Jerry Lee Lewis, Chuck Berry and Little Richard over and over." When he became a professional musician, he would always return to the songs of his youth when jamming with other musicians. Partly because he was never a confident guitarist and the rock 'n' roll songs of his youth were seared into his memory, but also because they meant so much to him. Rock 'n' roll meant fun and during his "lost weekend" he recorded an album of oldies simply for the pleasure it gave him. Although he developed an interest in other types of music, he always returned to rock 'n' roll.

It was inevitable that Lennon would form and lead his own group. The Quarrymen skiffle group developed from his circle of school friends, and he took it very seriously. He was constantly on the lookout for new and better musicians to improve the group. Nothing was going to stand in his way when it came to his music and the group's future success. When he met Paul McCartney at Saint Peter's Church Fete, he knew he could only improve the group, and so he was in. The addition of George Harrison was also for the betterment of the group. The only concession Lennon ever made was the inclusion of his best friend, Stuart Sutcliffe. It was one of the few occasions when he let his heart rule his head. Sutcliffe was not a natural musician; the fact that he'd won enough money to buy a bass guitar had some influence on Lennon's decision, but it was friendship that finally convinced him.

Lennon met Sutcliffe at Liverpool College of Art. A quiet intellectual, Sutcliffe was a gifted artist and every inch Lennon's opposite. Lennon's first wife, Cynthia, summed up their friendship. "It was a very beautiful relationship John had with Stu. It was like John was Ying and he was Yang. Stuart had the discipline, the talent, he was a genius in his own right. John was the outrageous musician, who Stuart was fascinated by, and Stuart taught John many things. They totally understood each other and gave to each other what they knew, what they had to offer. John helped Stuart to assert himself, and Stuart helped John to come down a little bit, to be less abrasive, less harsh." It was the kind of relationship that Lennon formed again and again. Many of his closest friends, his manager, wives and lovers all blossomed thanks to his influence but, more often than not, were his opposite in intellect, talent and character.

Whatever he displayed on the outside wasn't necessarily the truth. His violent outbursts concealed deep rooted emotional insecurity; he was a hard man who was as likely to receive beatings as give them and a drunk who couldn't hold his drink. Paul McCartney shared Lennon's interests and recognized his weaknesses: "John was more introverted and more willing to hurt in order to save his own neck... John had a lot to guard against, and it formed his personality; he was a very guarded person. I think that was the balance between us: John was caustic and witty out of necessity and, underneath, quite a warm character when you got to know him."

Lennon quickly established himself at college; his contemporaries remember his physical presence rather than his intellectual capacity. Since losing his mother, he'd hardened and was often aggressive, both verbally and physically. Several of his fellow students found him frightening and were cautious in his company. He had a reputation among teachers for being disruptive, and was known to use his fists to win an argument. He used violence to mask his insecurities and the emotional pain he experienced at the death of his mother. Although he was both an artist and a musician, he often chose to express himself by attacking the weaknesses he saw in others.

He was, however, intelligent, humorous and attractive. Despite his rough veneer, he made an impact with the girls and had a brief relationship with fellow student, Thelma Pickles, before meeting his future wife Cynthia Powell. Shy, polite and well spoken, Powell was the opposite of Lennon in almost every respect. Initially, Lennon hid his infatuation by attacking her middle-class background. It was the only way he knew of dealing with his own inadequacies. His Aunt Mimi suggested that he was as frightened of Cynthia as she was of him. But while Cynthia feared his violent outbursts, Lennon was an emotional poltroon. His inability to show any emotion may have been a consequence of his upbringing. Although his Aunt Mimi loved him dearly, she could be cold and distant and found it difficult to show her emotions.

Lennon continued to concentrate his energies on his group rather than his art, and in 1960 the group secured the first of several engagements in Hamburg, Germany. By now John had settled on a new name, The Beatles, and Hamburg was where they came of age. Freed from the restraints and responsibilities he had at home, Lennon could indulge himself. He began drinking heavily, took copious amounts of Preludin – a powerful amphetamine-based slimming pill – and got paid for playing rock 'n' roll all night long. Here he could be as outrageous as he liked and delighted in ridiculing the German audience. The long hours on stage transformed The Beatles from rough and ready amateurs into a tight rock 'n' roll group. "We got better and got more confidence," remembered Lennon. "We couldn't help it, with all the experience, playing all night long." Things were beginning to look up for Lennon and The Beatles. The Beatles returned to Hamburg in June 1961 and this time made a record. Or rather, they backed Tony Sheridan on recordings he made for Bert Kaempfert, and recorded two songs that remained unreleased until they became famous. Naturally, Lennon sang lead on one of his favorite oldies, "Ain't She Sweet," and the group recorded an instrumental written by Lennon and Harrison, "Cry For A Shadow." Sheridan's recording of the traditional song, "My Bonnie," with The Beatles backing him was released in Germany and copies found their way to Liverpool where they were played in local clubs. The Beatles were by now big news on Merseyside and thanks to a young man asking for a copy of the record they'd made in Germany, came to the notice of Brian Epstein.

The man who would become The Beatles' manager first saw them at The Cavern club. They were rough and ready, but he knew they had something. Within weeks he'd offered to manage them. Epstein's plan to make

22 **Lennon on the set of The Beatles'**

first full-length feature film, *A Hard*

Day's Night.

them superstars was simple: clean them up, put them in suits and stopped them eating on stage. Although it meant selling out, Lennon was happy to go along with the plan. "Epstein said, 'Look if you wear a suit... you'll get this much money'... all right wear a suit. I'll wear a suit. I'll wear a bloody balloon if somebody's going to pay me." Phase two of Epstein's plan was to secure them a recording contract. This was more difficult than he expected. Only Decca Records showed any interest, and then only because Epstein's record shops were the biggest record retailer in the North East and it didn't want to upset him. Decca offered the group an audition at its London studio on January 1, 1962, which they failed. Epstein managed to book them on to some BBC Radio programs, but a record contract with one of the big four national record companies looked remote.

In June 1962, Epstein finally convinced George Martin, who managed EMI subsidiary Parlophone Records, to sign the group. It was their charisma and a song written by Lennon and McCartney, "Love Me Do," that persuaded him. However, Martin was unhappy with The Beatles' drummer, Pete Best, which led to him being sacked. The group already had their eye on the drummer with the Liverpool group Rory Storm and The Hurricanes. Like McCartney and Harrison before him, Starr was chosen because he would improve their sound. Starr might have joined The Beatles but Martin still wasn't impressed and booked a session musician for the group's first proper recording session at EMI Studios, Abbey Road, and Starr was left to rattle a tambourine.

At about the same time as The Beatles signed with EMI, Cynthia Powell became pregnant. Lennon did the decent thing and they married on August 23. "I said, yes, we have to get married. I didn't fight it." he recalled. "When I told Aunt Mimi she just let out a groan." Now he was on the cusp of becoming a star, his marriage and Cynthia's pregnancy had to be kept a secret from fans. Cynthia gave birth to their son, Julian, in April 1963, only weeks after The Beatles scored their first Number One single with "Please Please Me." By the end of the year, The Beatles were national stars. "She Loves You" became the biggest selling single in Britain in 1963. In October, the group played the London Palladium and caused a sensation when the surrounding streets were blocked by hundreds of screaming fans. Reported in the national newspapers the following day, Beatlemania was born.

Although The Beatles were big news at home, success elsewhere took longer to achieve. In January 1964, they played 18 shows at the Olympia Theatre in Paris, where they faced an enthusiastic but mainly male audience. It was while in Paris that they learnt that their fifth single, "I Want To Hold Your Hand," had reached Number One in America. The Beatles had some minor success in America, but had been frustrated by Capitol Records' lack of interest. Capitol had passed on all their previous releases, which it considered un-commercial.

Few British recording artists had topped the American charts, so it had been up to independent record labels to issue the group's early records.

It had been a long, hard struggle but when success came in America it was on an unimaginable scale. Their records sold in millions, they sold millions of dollars of merchandise, and they were feted wherever they went. For Lennon it was everything he'd dreamt of. "Oh sure. I dug the fame, the power, the money, and playing big crowds. Conquering America was the best thing," he said. He admitted that none of The Beatles would have made it in America on their own; each played an important part in the group's success, but Lennon's articulate interviews and acerbic wit helped elevate The Beatles above the usual pop star banalities. Whenever The Beatles were interviewed, it was Lennon the journalists made for first.

On their return to England, The Beatles began work on their first film, *A Hard Day's Night*. Like everything else they did it broke the mold. No cheap exploitation movie for them, rather director Richard Lester fashioned a gritty, monochrome document of a day in their life that was as fast paced and witty as they were. The British edition of the soundtrack album featured 13 Lennon/McCartney songs, which was a first, and a remarkable testament to their stamina and talents as songwriters. Hailed as the greatest songwriters since Schubert, their songs weren't only hits for The Beatles, but for artists as diverse as Ella Fitzgerald and Peter Sellers. Aunt Mimi's remark that Lennon would never make money from the guitar now sounded hollow indeed.

While The Beatles were busy making *A Hard Day's Night,* Lennon somehow managed to find time to publish his first book, *In His Own Write.* Much of the material was drawn from the *Daily Howl* comics he'd drawn as a child. A short volume of poems and humorous drawings, it found Lennon compared to Joyce and Thurber. Naturally he was delighted, for if nothing else it validated his claims that he knew from an early age that he was destined for greatness. It also revealed something of Lennon's darker side and the trauma he experienced as an adolescent. Populated by cripples, cruelly deformed creatures and the kind of sick humor that only a few years previously would have got Lenny Bruce arrested, Lennon said of the characters he created, "I suppose they were manifestations of hidden cruelties. They were very Alice in Wonderland and Winnie the Pooh. I was very hung up then. I got rid of a lot of that. It was my version of what was happening then."

Lennon was still haunted by events from his childhood and although The Beatles were the most successful entertainment phenomenon ever, he still suffered from self-doubt and low self-esteem. In the autumn of 1964, he recorded "I'm A Loser" for The Beatles' fourth album, *Beatles For Sale.* The following year he recorded the title song for their second film, *Help!* He later said, "I meant it – it was real. The lyric is as good as it was then. It was no different, and it made me feel secure to know that I was that aware of myself then." The song obviously resonated with Lennon because he returned to it in 1970 when he was in primal therapy, and considered re-recording it on several other occasions.

Blessed with one of the greatest rock voices ever, Lennon disliked hearing his own voice. The misgivings that affected his writing also had an impact on the way his voice was recorded. Once he discovered that he could make his voice sound different by "double tracking" or adding echo to it he insisted it be smothered in effects. As studio technology progressed, Lennon went to great lengths to disguise his voice. With the dawn of psychedelia, it became increasingly distorted until it reached its most altered state on The Beatles' masterpiece "Tomorrow Never Knows." Reservations about his voice never left him. During his last recording session in 1980, he spent more time perfecting his vocals than any other aspect of the recording process.

The Beatles workload was unparalleled. There was always pressure to write more songs, a relentless round of recording sessions, radio and television appearances, feature-films and an unrelenting demand for live appearances. With demands like this something was bound to give. Much of what they were recording was impossible to reproduce on stage, and because they were playing stadiums they couldn't hear themselves anyway. Their world tour of 1966, which took in Germany, Japan, the Philippines and America, was the straw that broke the camel's back. Touring wasn't fun anymore. Everywhere they went there were protests, death threats, and crowds of fans that the group's security was unable to control. On top of this Lennon caused controversy in America when a statement he made in a British newspaper was taken out of context.

Speaking to Maureen Cleave in the *London Evening* Standard, he made a remark about Christianity's inability to engage young people and compared the popularity of The Beatles to that of Christ. The remark went unnoticed in Britain where it was quoted within the context of a knowledgeable article in which he spoke at length about subjects beyond the scope of most pop stars. Four months later, it was reproduced out of context in an American magazine aimed at teenage girls and caused outrage across the country. Radio stations banned The Beatles' records, public bonfires were organized of Beatles records and merchandise, the Ku Klux Klan even got involved. Lennon was made to feel very uncomfortable and forced to apologize during The Beatles final tour of America. At every press conference The Beatles gave, he was asked to explain his remarks, which he did with growing annoyance. "I'm not anti-God, anti-Christ or anti-religion," he said. "I was not saying we are greater or better. I believe in God, but not as one thing, not as an old man in the sky. I believe that what people call God is something in all of us."

It was the end of The Beatles as a touring group, but the making of Lennon the peacemaker. When The Beatles returned to Britain they took a break and embarked on solo projects. Lennon was offered the part of Private Gripweed in Richard Lester's anti-war film, *How I Won the War.* He'd wanted to speak out against the Vietnam War for some time, but had been stopped by Brian Epstein, who still considered The Beatles little more than a pop group. *How I Won the War* showed Lennon that there was a role for him outside of The Beatles and that he could play a positive part in the growing peace movement. "I hate war," he said. "The Vietnam War and all that is being done there made me feel like that. If there is another war, I won't fight – and although the youngsters may be asked to fight, I'll stand up there and try and stop them." However, before he could fully engage with the peace movement, he had The Beatles' next album to record.

Freed from the demands of touring, The Beatles moved into EMI Studios and began recording what many believe to be their greatest album, *Sgt. Pepper's Lonely Hearts Club Band.* The first song they recorded was Lennon's "Strawberry Fields Forever" and its recording set the standard for the rest of the album. Unhappy with his first attempt at the song, Lennon insisted that they record a second version in a higher key and faster tempo, onto which George Martin added his score. However, Lennon wasn't happy with this either and asked Martin to splice the first part of the earlier version together with the new faster version. The Beatles were pushing their creativity and technology to its limits. They spent 700 hours recording *Sgt. Pepper's Lonely Hearts Club Band,* an unprecedented length of time, and transformed the recording studio into an experimental sound laboratory.

Lennon's writing was becoming increasingly oblique. "Strawberry Fields Forever" was more than a song about childhood memories of Liverpool; it was his way of saying that he saw the world differently from others who lived with their eyes closed. If previously he perceived the world differently from others, now it was skewed by LSD. It certainly influenced his songwriting, but when people noticed that the first letters of the nouns in "Lucy In The Sky With Diamonds" spelt LSD, he rejected the idea that it was a pro-drug song. It didn't stop the BBC from banning it and his masterpiece "A Day in the Life," because of the phrase "I'd love to turn you on." Lennon didn't want to turn people onto LSD, he wanted to open their minds to their potential and ability to affect social change. If he failed to communicate this with "A Day in the Life," he was more successful with the song he wrote for The Beatles appearance on the first global television broadcast, *Our World.*

Commissioned by the BBC to write a simple song that could be understood by viewers everywhere, Lennon fashioned a song that summarized his growing belief in the power of people to bring about positive change and his desire for peace. "All You Need Is Love" was in many ways a precursor to "Imagine." Lennon tells his listeners, "there's nothing you can do that can't be done" and what's more, doing it was easy. If "Strawberry Fields Forever" appeared ambivalent, "it doesn't matter much to me," "All You Need Is Love" sent out a positive message that asked people to consider their collective potential and strive for a world that placed love and peace above war and destruction.

28 Lennon returned to New
York City in 1974 to record his
Walls And Bridges album.

with help from Elton John, it
featured his first solo number 1
single "Whatever Gets You Thru

"All You Need Is Love" was Lennon's first step to becoming an ambassador for peace, but before he could fully devote himself to the cause he'd need to find some inner peace of his own. Introduced to the teachings of Maharishi Mahesh Yogi by George Harrison, he thought he'd found it in Transcendental Meditation (TM). Initially, he saw it as a force for good, but he quickly became disillusioned and wrote a thinly veiled attack on the Maharishi, in the form of the song "Sexy Sadie." While immersed in TM, Lennon's world was rocked by two events. The Beatles' manager, Brian Epstein, died and threw the group into a traumatic freefall that would eventually lead to its end. At the same time his interest in the conceptual artist, Yoko Ono, whom he'd met the previous year, was pricked by her "Birthday Festival Event," during which she sent him, a card everyday for 13 days that instructed him to "Breathe" or "Dance." By the early summer of 1968 Lennon had ditched the Maharishi and started a relationship with Ono.

"I always had this dream of meeting an artist, an artist girl who would be like me," he said. "And I thought it was a myth, but then I met Yoko, and that was it." Ono transformed Lennon; she filled him with confidence, inspiration and energy. Lennon threw himself into her world of avant-garde art and together they dedicated much of their energies to promoting peace. "We both tried to find something we had in common, a common goal in life," he said. "We decided the thing we had in common was love, and from love came peace, so we decided to work for world peace."

He became more overtly political, writing "Revolution" and the Ono-inspired "Revolution 9" for The Beatles' *White Album*. The two were inseparable; they went everywhere together, including Beatles recording sessions – she sang on "The Continuing Story of Bungalow Bill" – which upset the already fragile group dynamics. Lennon also made his first solo musical appearance outside The Beatles, naturally with Ono in support, and appeared on The Rolling Stones' ill-fated *Rock 'n' Roll Circus.*

Lennon, with Ono's encouragement, was drifting apart from The Beatles. With Ono he'd found his ideal partner, she inspired him to even greater creative heights and his celebrity status ensured that everything they did made headline news. When they married on March 20, 1969, it made perfect sense to use the publicity to do something positive.

At last, Lennon had finally committed himself to the kind of political activism that had gripped Europe and America in the previous year. 1968 had been a year of protests and riots against the Vietnam War. Lennon had written about his desire for revolution, but had been unable to commit to the idea because of its too often violent nature.

With Ono, he'd found a non-violent way to protest, make himself and his cause heard, and promote world peace.

Their crusade for peace and an end to the Vietnam War took a giant leap when they turned their honeymoon into a vast media circus to promote their cause. From then on they became living works of art working in the name of peace. "Our life is our art," said Lennon. "That's what the bed-ins were. In effect, we were doing a commercial for peace on the front of the papers instead of a commercial for war."

The Lennons wanted a cultural revolution that encouraged self-realization and personal projection; a revolution that came from the people not leaders. Like Bob Dylan before him, Lennon was saying don't follow leaders, the revolution starts on an individual level and builds from there. By using music and art as building blocks, the Lennons hoped to encourage people to use their potential to build a global utopia. The problem was that most people didn't see how staying in bed for a week or growing one's hair would bring about peace. The truth was that Lennon and Ono were too cerebral for most to grasp what they were trying to achieve. Although his solo career was well established, he'd already issued two solo albums with Ono, and on his return to Britain he began work on The Beatles final album, *Abbey Road.* However, by September he'd decided that the time had come to leave the group. Although he told the other Beatles of his decision, he kept it from the press.

In 1969, *Rolling Stone* magazine voted Lennon man of the year, and British sociologist and anthropologist Dr Desmond Morris went one better and made him man of the decade – John F Kennedy and Ho Chi Minh were the other contenders for the title. While Lennon was being considered as influential as some of the most powerful leaders the world had ever seen, his views were becoming more radical. He remained a fervent pacifist, but as the Vietnam War escalated, his views became increasingly left-wing. Lennon was fast becoming the king of counterculture, and was happy to donate his money or time to what he considered worthy causes. Lennon and Ono ended the year with a global poster campaign that announced "WAR IS OVER! IF YOU WANT IT Happy Christmas from John & Yoko." This simple, yet powerful, idea recalled Ono's earlier conceptual instructional art works and kept their peace campaign in the public eye.

1970 was a year of change for Lennon. On April 10, Paul McCartney announced that he had left The Beatles. Lennon never forgave him for it. Not because he'd wanted to keep the group going, he didn't, but because he'd started the group and wanted to be the one to announce its demise. 1970 also saw the Lennons retreat from the glare of publicity. The time had come for Lennon to deal with the pain he'd suffered at his mother's death. In April he flew to Los Angeles to undertake three months of intensive primal therapy under Dr Arthur Janov. During his stay, he attempted to come to terms with his anger and pain, which spilled out of him and into the songs he wrote while he was in therapy.

The songs he wrote while in Los Angeles formed what many consider to be his greatest solo work, *John Lennon/Plastic Ono Band*. The album found him back in the studio with Ringo Starr and bassist, Klaus Voormann, whom he'd first met in Hamburg. The album was stark, raw and personal. An unashamedly cathartic piece of work, it found Lennon offering his soul to the world. Few rock stars have produced anything as personal and moving as this album. It closes with "My Mummy's Dead," an ethereal ballad in which Lennon finally laid the ghost of his mother to rest.

The Lennons spent the early part of 1971 in Japan with Ono's family, but had to cut short their stay because of the impending court case to wind up The Beatles. On his return to Britain, Lennon gave an interview to a left-wing magazine, *Red Mole,* after which he wrote "Power to the People." "The left wing talk about giving the power to the people," he said. "Everybody knows that the people have the power, all we have to do is awaken the power in the people." That's what he'd been trying to do in more subtle ways for years, but now he began to align himself, albeit cautiously, with radical left-wing politics. He was, however, still unsure whether or not to fully commit himself because his next album wasn't so much a call to arms as it was an invitation to dream.

On his previous album Lennon said "the dream is over," its follow-up offered a new dream, a dream of a world united in peace and harmony; a world where everyone was equal, regardless of color, creed, class, race or wealth. The title song, "Imagine" was inspired by Ono's instruction pieces – works of art that only become a reality when they are realized by others. Lennon took her idea and wrote a song of hope for the world. He believed that if everyone imagined a better world that's what we'd have. Later, Ono would paraphrase the song's main idea with the aphorism "A dream you dream alone is only a dream. A dream you dream together is reality." "Imagine" asks us to see ourselves as people of the world, not as individuals defined by nationhood, religion or possessions. Of course, Lennon was criticized for the line "imagine no possessions," but what he was saying was try and imagine a world without the things that define us, and that includes the things we own.

"Imagine" would define Lennon and his beliefs. It become his best known song and is one of the top 100 most performed songs of all time. In 2004, *Rolling Stone* magazine voted it one of the greatest song of all time. Lennon and Ono finished recording the *Imagine* album in New York City, and by September they'd moved to the city for good. On his arrival, Lennon was met by Jerry Rubin and Abbie Hoffman, leaders of the Youth International Party (Yippie), and began working with them on various political protests. Lennon and the Elephant's Memory band performed benefit concerts for the White Panther Party leader John Sinclair, for victims of the shootings at Attica State Prison, and for more mainstream causes such as the *Jerry Lewis Telethon.*

The Lennons were now fully engaged freedom fighters. Naturally they wrote about their activities and the changes they hoped would result from them. Lennon began writing in earnest, but where he'd previously written from his heart, his latest batch of songs merely recorded what was happening around him. The ensuing album, *Some Time In New York City,* lacked the emotional impact of his previous albums and didn't fare well with the critics. Neither was it well received by the U.S. government.

The administration of President Nixon considered Lennon a disrupting influence and wanted him gone. The FBI tapped his telephones, followed his every move and even analyzed his lyrics. It attempted to have him deported citing a previous conviction for possession of cannabis. Lennon was about to face his greatest battle with authority, it would drag on for years and affect his relationship with Ono and his work. When Nixon was re-elected, Lennon distanced himself from radical left-wing politics and concentrated on his career as a musician. His next album, *Mind Games,* contained fewer overtly political songs, but its title song restated his desire for peaceful revolution, albeit with an ambiguous, spiritual overtone not dissimilar to that of "Imagine."

The strain the Lennons had put themselves through began to take its toll on their relationship. Not long after the release of the *Mind Games* album, Lennon and Ono separated and Lennon moved to Los Angeles. Hanging out with some of rock's heavyweight drinkers, Lennon reverted to the rock 'n' roll hedonist of the Hamburg days. "In LA you either have to be down on the beach or you become part of that never-ending show-business party circuit," he said. "That scene makes me nervous and when I get nervous I have to have a drink and when I drink I get aggressive." It was as if the years of campaigning and primal therapy had never happened. The separation caused him a lot of pain and he tried to mask it by turning to drink. It was the start of what he called his "lost weekend," a weekend that lasted 18 months and saw him back in the newspapers for all the wrong reasons.

One of the reasons Lennon moved to Los Angeles was to record an album of his favorite rock 'n' roll oldies with producer Phil Spector. The maverick producer had co-produced Lennon's previous three albums, but Lennon had always managed to control his excesses. On this occasion, however, Lennon was as out of control as Spector. The recording sessions were as chaotic as Lennon's lifestyle at that time, and were brought to an abrupt end when Spector disappeared with the master tapes. With little else to do, Lennon offered to produce an album with his drinking buddy, Harry Nilsson. These sessions were no less chaotic, but they did see Lennon reunited in the studio with his former songwriting partner, Paul McCartney. Lennon struggled to finish Nilsson's album in Los Angeles, and realizing that the hedonism wasn't going to stop, he returned to New York City to complete the album. With Nilsson's album finished, Lennon began work on a new album of his own, *Walls And Bridges.* Working with Elton John, he recorded his first number 1 single, "Whatever Gets You Thru The Night" and appeared alongside the pianist at Madison Square Garden on November 28 – his last ever live performance.

Backstage he was reunited with Ono, and before long he'd moved back into their apartment at the Dakota building. "When [Yoko and I] got back together, we decided that this was our life," he said. "That having a baby was important to us, and that everything else was subsidiary to that, and that therefore everything else had to be abandoned. I mean abandonment gave us the fulfillment we were looking for and the space to breathe…"

Despite the success of *Walls And Bridges* Lennon considered it "the work of a semi-slick craftsman." For him it was clouded by the depression he'd experienced at being separated from Ono, the constant threat of deportation and The Beatles' continuing business woes. "Musically, my mind was just a clutter," he said. "There was no inspiration and it gave an aura of misery…"

As depressed as he was, Lennon obviously enjoyed being back in the recording studio. In January 1975, he recorded two songs with David Bowie for his *Young Americans* album, one of which, "Fame," he co-wrote. It would become Bowie's first American number 1 record. Revitalized by his return to Manhattan, Lennon began recording more rock 'n' roll oldies for the album he'd started the previous year with Spector. Issued in early 1975, *Rock 'n' Roll* was the last set of new Lennon recordings he'd issue for five years.

October 1975 was a landmark month for the Lennons. On October 7, Lennon finally won his battle with the American government and had his deportation order revoked. (He was finally granted his green card on July 27, 1976). Two days later, on his 35th birthday, Ono gave birth to their son, Sean. To celebrate his birth and the end of his contract with EMI, Lennon compiled a best of album, *Shaved Fish,* that drew a line under his solo recording career so far.

Although he was now a free agent, Lennon began planning a new album, but soon abandoned any idea of continuing his recording career to devote the next five years of his life to bringing up Sean. Lennon had grown tired of the music business and used the birth of his son to withdraw from the public gaze. He may have become a "househusband," but that didn't stop the creative juices from flowing. He regained his appetite for books and read widely on ancient history and religion. He kept a personal diary and wrote prose in the style of his first two books, published posthumously as *Skywriting by Word of Mouth.* He also continued to write songs, although with no deadline to focus his attention, his output slowed considerably.

Lennon's time as a "househusband" wasn't always easy, but on May 27, 1979, John and Yoko placed a full page letter in the *New York Times* that suggested that the hard times were finally over. "The house is getting very comfortable now. Sean is beautiful. The plants are growing. The cats are purring. The town is shining, sun, rain or snow. We live in a beautiful universe." As idyllic as their lives seemed, they hadn't forgotten that at heart they were campaigners for social equality. The letter continued, "If two people like us can do what we are doing with our lives, any miracle is possible! The future of the earth is up to all of us."

In June 1980, Lennon sailed to Bermuda aboard the 43-foot Megan Jaye. The voyage and subsequent sojourn on Bermuda reawakened his desire to record, and with Sean's fifth birthday on the horizon, the time was right to make plans for his comeback. Inspired by his surroundings, he composed a batch of new songs and reworked some he'd been working on but hadn't finished. The new album would be a joint John and Yoko release, their first since 1972, and was the first in a planned trilogy that would culminate with a world tour. While in Bermuda, Lennon visited a botanical garden and spotted an orchid named "Double Fantasy," it was the perfect title for the album he planned to record on his return to Manhattan. Lennon and Ono began recording in August with a hand-picked group of session musicians. When the Lennons confirmed that they were back in the studio it made headlines around the world. Expectations were high and Lennon knew he had to come up with something special after such a long silence. The album was preceded by the single "(Just Like) Starting Over," a song that found Lennon referencing his early rock 'n' roll influences and suggesting that this was the beginning of a new phase in his life. *Double Fantasy* followed to mixed reviews; it wasn't representative of the acidic Lennon of old, but as far as he was concerned its message was consistent with previous albums. "The consciousness is, 'Let's see what we shall pray for together. Let's make it stronger by picturing the same image'. And that is the secret. Because you can be together but projecting different things."

With the release of *Double Fantasy* came a wave of publicity, the Lennons giving major interviews to *Newsweek*, *Playboy* and the BBC. On the morning of December 8, they gave a lengthy interview to RKO to promote the album, and later returned to the recording studio to finish work on Ono's "Walking On Thin Ice." Lennon had high hopes for the song and planned for Ono to release it as a single. The couple left the recording studio at 10.30pm with the intention of getting something to eat before returning to the Dakota. However, they decided to go directly home instead because they wanted to see Sean before going to a restaurant.

Earlier in the day, Lennon had given his autograph to a fan. Unknown to him the young man, had remained at the Dakota awaiting his return. That night the Lennons limousine pulled up at the curb rather than drive into the courtyard, and as Lennon crossed the sidewalk, the mentally disturbed young man shot him five times in the back. That somebody who campaigned so intensely for peace should meet such a violent death shocked the world. This senseless, cowardly act did more than rob the world of a musician, it deprived it of a remarkable human being who touched the lives of millions. A musician, a writer, an artist, a film maker, an activist, a father, a dreamer, Lennon did everything with a passion that inspired others. His spirit lives on in everyone who imagines a world without prejudice, hunger and war.

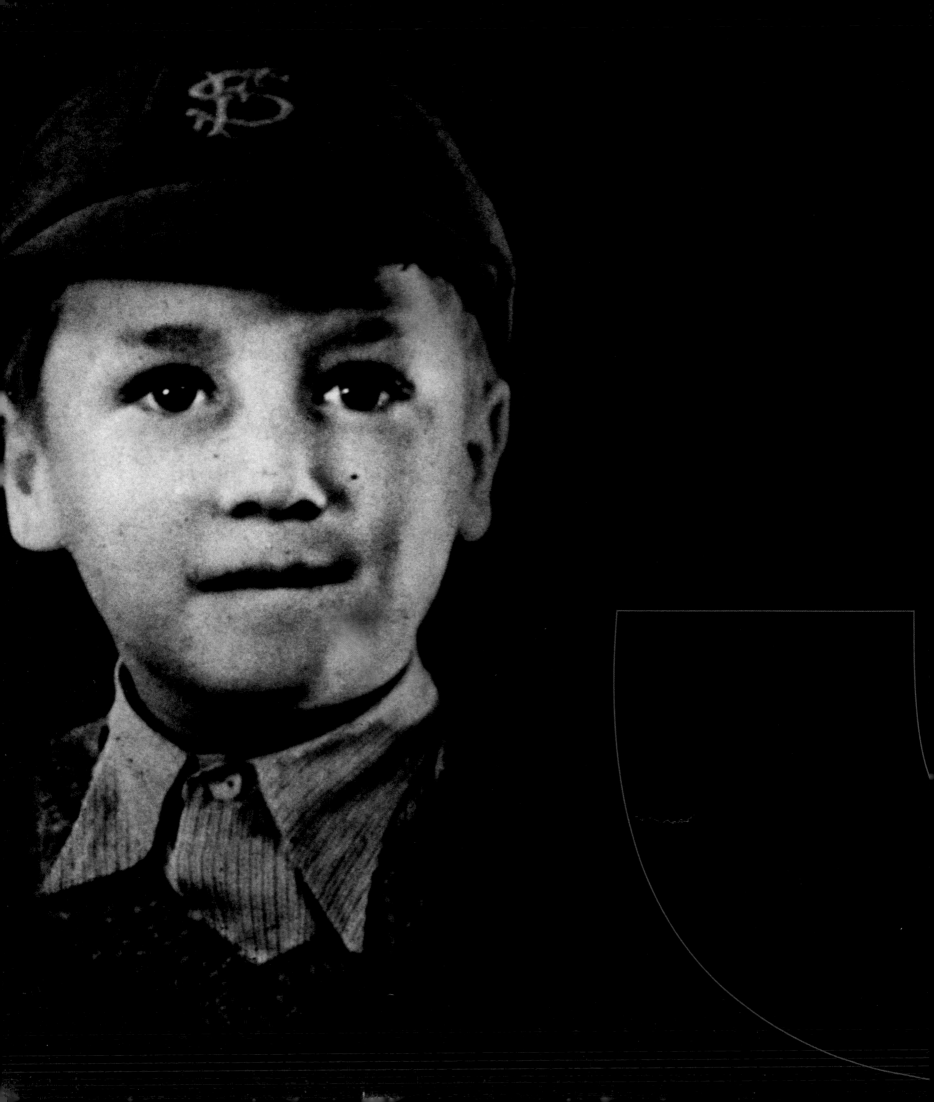

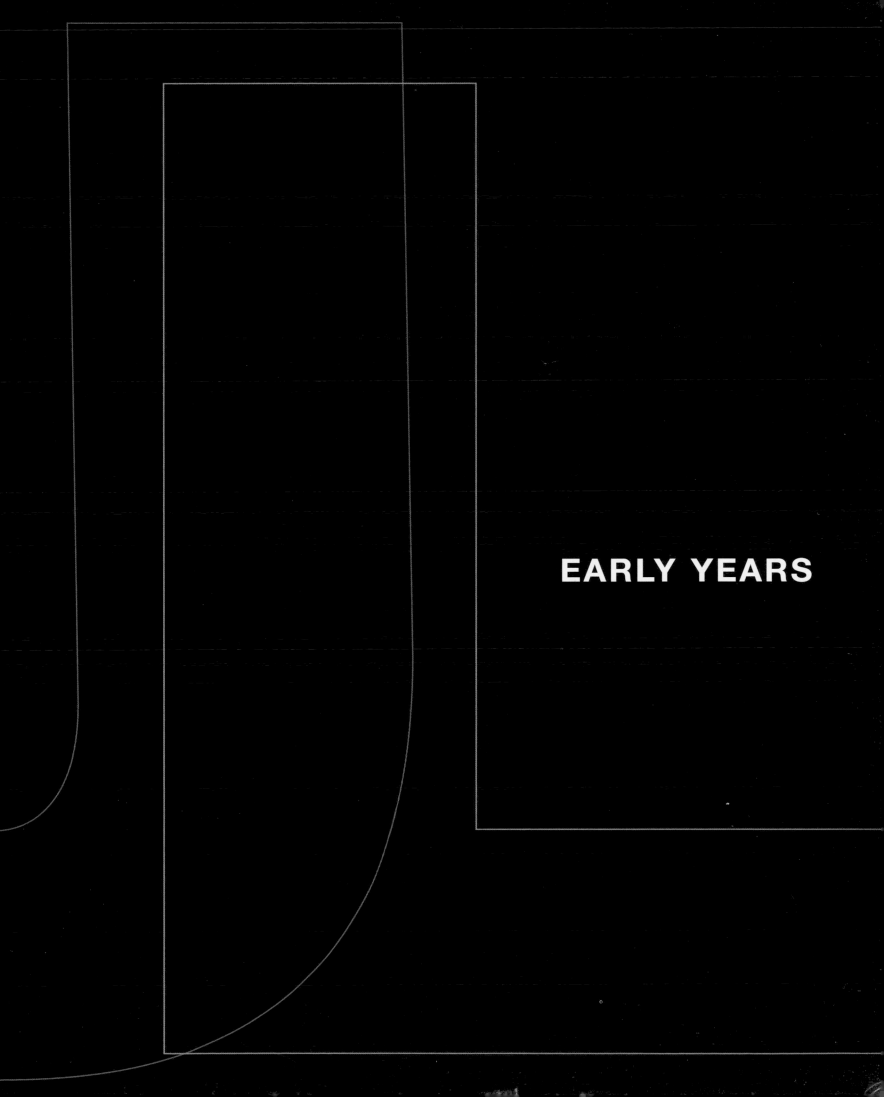

EARLY YEARS

CERTIFIED COPY OF AN ENTRY OF BIRTH

The statutory fee for this certificate is 3s. 9d.
Where a search is necessary to find the entry,
a search fee is payable in addition.

REGISTRATION DISTRICT _Liverpool South._

__1940.__ **BIRTH in the Sub-district of** _Abercromby_ in

Columns:—	1	2	3	4	5	6
No.	When and where born	Name, if any	Sex	Name, and surname of father	Name, surname, and maiden surname of mother	Occupation of father
483.	Ninth October 1940. Liverpool Maternity Hospital 49.	John Winston	Boy	Alfred Lennon	Julia Lennon formerly Stanley	Steward (Steamship) 9. Newcastle Road Liverpool 15.

CERTIFIED to be a true copy of an entry in the certified copy of a Register of Births in the District a

Given at the GENERAL REGISTER OFFICE, SOMERSET HOUSE, LONDON, under the Seal of the said Office, the

BC 642560

GIVEN AT THE GENERAL REGISTER OFFICE, SOMERSET HOUSE, LONDON.

Application Number .... 652 300 ....

the _County Borough of Liverpool_

	7	8	9	10*
	Signature, description, and residence of informant	When registered	Signature of registrar	Name entered after registration
	J. Lennon. Father			
	Newcastle Road Liverpool 15.	Eleventh November 1940.	J.R. Kirkwood Registrar	—

*See note overleaf.

mentioned.

18ᵗʰ day of _July_ 19⁶⁸.

Register Office shall be received as evidence of the birth
in the said Office shall be of any force or effect unless it

, knowing it to be false, is liable to prosecution.

38-39 John Winston Lennon was born at Liverpool Maternity Hospital and named after his paternal grandfather and Winston Churchill. His father, Alfred, was not present at the birth because he was at sea.

41 A pensive John, age six. He had recently experienced the trauma of having to choose between living with his mother or father. He chose his father, but when Julia walked away he ran crying after her.

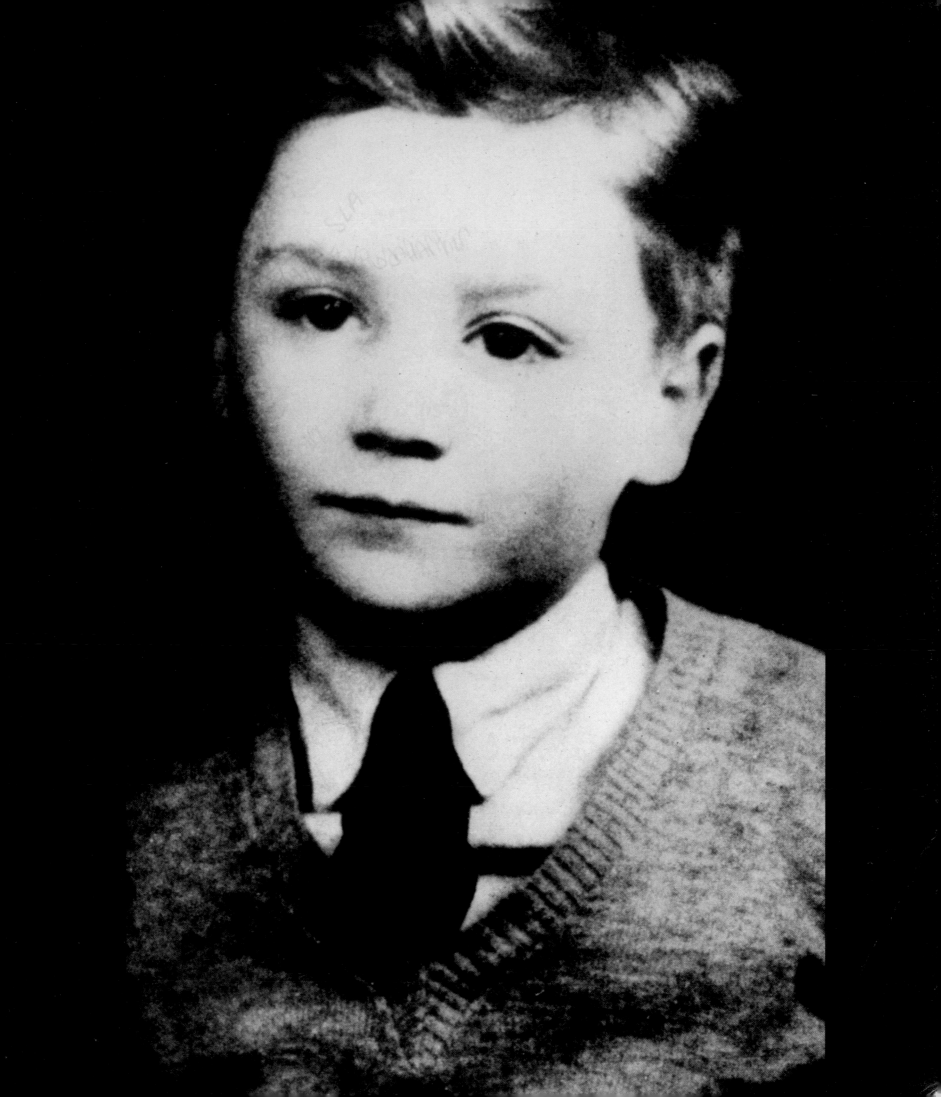

EARLY YEARS

John Winston Lennon was born in Liverpool on October 9, 1940, the first son of Alfred and Julia Lennon. Married in 1938, they saw little of one another. Alfred Lennon, a ship's steward, set sail for the West Indies the day after they were married, and was seldom home. When Julia discovered that she was pregnant, she was unable to contact her husband to tell him the news. Britain was at war with Germany, U-boats hunted merchant shipping in the Atlantic and the port of Liverpool was a prime target for Luftwaffe bombing raids. However, the myth that Lennon was born during an air raid is entirely that, a myth. There was no raid on Liverpool that night.

Unable to cope on her own, Julia arranged for her son to be brought up by her sister, Mimi Elizabeth Stanley Smith. From the age of five, Lennon was brought up by his Aunt Mimi and Uncle George at 251 Menlove Avenue in the leafy suburb of Woolton. Mimi and George raised the child as their own. Uncle George taught him to read from newspapers, and he soon developed a love of books, which he devoured with a passion.

At the age of five, Lennon began attending Dovedale Primary school, a three mile bus journey from his home. He was a bright, creative young boy with a strong personality. It was obvious he was different from the other boys, some of whom found him a little intimidating. Despite Mimi's strict discipline, Lennon often found himself in trouble when playing the class clown.

As bright as he was, Lennon was not academically gifted. A square peg in a round hole, when he started Quarry Bank Grammar School in the late summer of 1952, the rebelliousness that would make him a hero to millions was already well developed. Instead of homework, he spent his time writing and drawing in his exercise books. His imagination ran wild, and the resulting Daily Howl was passed round the classroom to disrupt and enliven lessons.

Two things happened to Lennon in 1955 that would influence the rest of his life. He heard Lonnie Donegan's recording of "Rock Island Line" and, more importantly, re-established a relationship with his mother. Julia was frivolous, the exact opposite of her serious sister. She encouraged her son's interest in music, teaching him some chords on the banjo and his first song, Buddy Holly's "That'll Be The Day." It was an important time for Lennon. He was establishing a relationship with his mother, developing as an individual and taking his first steps to becoming a musician.

While in his final year at Quarry Bank High School, Lennon acquired a guitar and formed his first group. Formed in March 1957 with his best friend, Pete Shotton, they were called The Blackjacks, but Lennon quickly changed it to The Quarrymen. Skiffle led him further from the academic path. But when he heard Elvis Presley, he'd never be the same again. "It was Elvis Presley all day long," remembered Mimi.

Mimi detested Lennon's infatuation with the guitar, she made him practice in the porch and told him, "The guitar's all very well, but you'll never make a living from it." That didn't stop him from playing the instrument at every opportunity. The Quarrymen often performed free of charge at school dances and became the talk of the school. They secured engagements at church halls and youth clubs, where they played the popular hits of the day, and in July 1957 were booked to play at St Peter's garden fete. They gave two performances, one in the afternoon in the garden and another in the church hall. Unknown to Lennon it was to be one of the most important days in his life.

A former member of The Quarrymen, Ivan Vaughan, brought his friend, James Paul McCartney, along to see the group perform. Lennon made a big impression on the 15-year-old McCartney, who was impressed with Lennon's ability to improvise new lyrics to the Del Vikings' "Come Go With Me." After the performance it was McCartney's turn to impress Lennon, which he did by playing Eddie Cochran's "Twenty Flight Rock." About a week later, McCartney bumped into Pete Shotton, who told him Lennon wanted him in the group.

In September 1957, Lennon enrolled at Liverpool College of Art. The soot blackened building was a stone's throw from the Liverpool Institute, where McCartney was studying. The two often spent their lunch breaks together, playing songs by Buddy Holly and the Everly Brothers. Occasionally, McCartney brought along his friend and rock 'n' roll obsessive, George Harrison, who would sit in on their lunch time practice sessions. Lennon was always looking to improve The Quarrymen, and recognized that Harrison's talent as a lead guitarist was exactly what they needed. The following year The Quarrymen made their first visit to a recording studio and cut two songs, "That'll Be The Day" and a McCartney / Harrison composition "In Spite Of All The Danger."

On July 15 1958, Lennon's world was shattered. Julia was killed by an off-duty police officer in a road traffic accident. Lennon carried the emotional scars for the rest of his life. They remained buried deep within him, only occasionally surfacing in his songs. It would take 12 years and a course of primal therapy before he came anywhere near to coming to terms with his mother's death, finally exorcising her ghost with the poignant "My Mummy's Dead."

43   Lennon, age seven, outside the front porch at Mendips. When he began learning the guitar, Mimi banished him to the porch saying "The guitar's all right as a hobby, John, but you'll never make a living with it."

45   John and his mother, Julia, enjoy the sunshine in the garden at his Aunt Mimi's house. During his childhood, John was surrounded by strong women who dotted on him. Aunt Mimi's motto for him was "Nothing but the finest."

46 top John's Aunt Mimi became his surrogate mother when her sister, Julia, left her son in her care. Although Mimi brought up John as if he were her own, Lennon rebelled against her middle class values and became an artist.

1952

46 bottom Uncle George delighted in spending his evenings reading the newspaper with John. Besides helping John to read, it became a habit that stayed with him for the rest of his life and informed some of his best loved lyrics.

46-47 Lennon, aged 10, with his neighbor's dog Squeaker in the back garden of Mimi and George's semi-detached house in the leafy suburbs of Liverpool. Despite later claims, Lennon's childhood was one of comfortable middle class contentment.

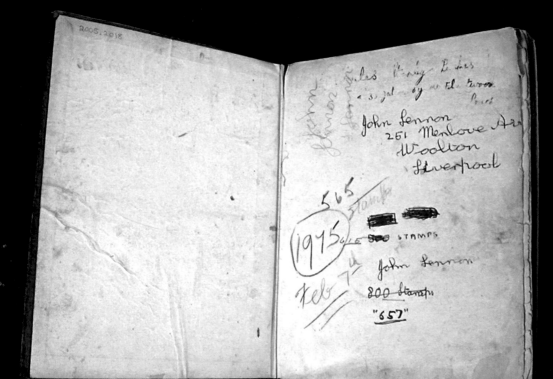

48 and 49 Lennon loved the bizarre characters and wordplay Lewis Carroll created for Alice In Wonderland, and couldn't resist illustrating his school books with brightly colored illustrations. He didn't enjoy school, but was incredibly creative. From the age of 12 he spent hours filling his exercise books with his own writing and drawings, which he titled the

FORM 1R.   SEPTEMBER 1952.

Smith.L.Lennon.Shotton.Jones.K.Beattie.Jackson.Jacobs.Walpole.Turner.Hamill.Fazakerley.Fox.
Anderson.Williams.Clemson.Brooke.Mr Burrows.Jones.P.Elliott.Rhind.Hillier.Rowley.
Callaway.Gooseman.Bolt.McEvoy.Norbury.Monchar.Jennett.Raisewell.

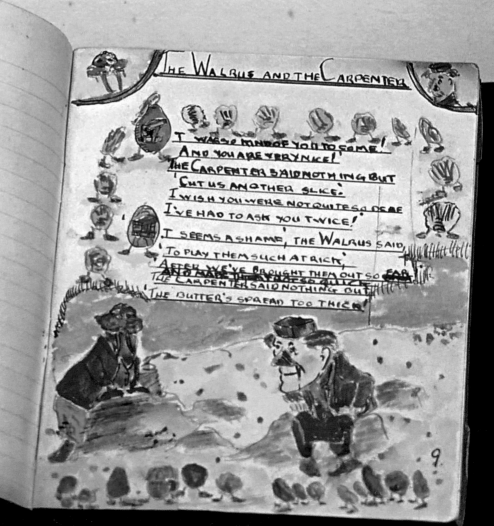

1955

50 George Harrison, John Lennon and Paul McCartney, The Quarrymen, pose for an early photograph. Inspired by the skiffle craze, Lennon formed The Quarrymen in 1957 while attending Quarry Bank High School.

1957

51 John Lennon met Paul McCartney at a performance The Quarrymen gave at St. Peter's Garden Fete in Woolton on July 6, 1957. Together they would become the most successful song writing partnership ever.

THE BEATLES' GOLDEN YEARS

54 In 1960, The Beatles made their first trip to Hamburg, Germany. Lennon had the time of his life living every teenagers dream. He got to meet some of his heroes, play loud rock 'n' roll and got paid for it. But he also missed Cynthia and Mimi.

56 George Harrison, John Lennon and Paul McCartney pose for their photograph outside the McCartney family home in Forthlin Road, Liverpool. It would be a further two years before Ringo Starr joined the group.

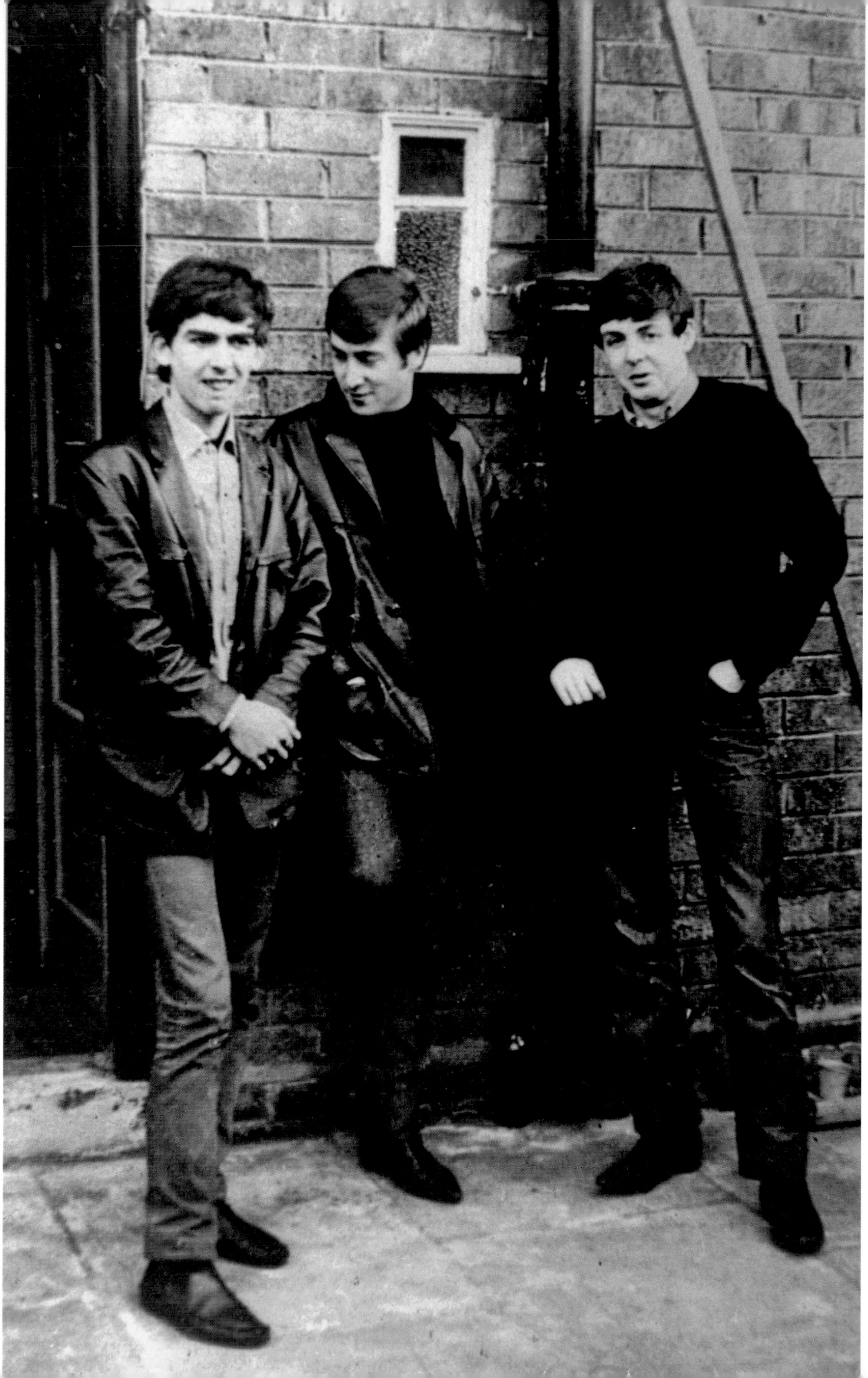

THE BEATLES' GOLDEN YEARS

The Beatles' debut single, "Love Me Do" was issued in Britain on Friday October 5 1962, four days before Lennon's 22nd birthday. It sold moderately well, for a group virtually unknown outside of the North East of England, and set The Beatles on their rapid rise to fame, something that had taken years to achieve.

Beginning in August 1960, The Beatles made several trips to Hamburg, Germany. It was here that their magic was forged. Audiences and club managers were demanding, and the long hours spent on stage transformed the inexperienced Liverpool lads into seasoned musicians.

In June 1961, they backed the English singer and guitarist Tony Sheridan at a recording session produced by Bert Kaempfert. "My Bonnie" was issued as a single in Germany and sold well in the Hamburg area. Few Liverpool groups had made a record, and its release changed their lives forever. In late October 1961, Raymond Jones entered North End Music Stores in Liverpool and asked for the record. The shop manager, Brian Epstein, prided himself on supplying his customers with any record they asked for and vowed to track it down. What's more, he was intrigued to learn that although the record was only available in Germany, The Beatles were a local group.

Some time later, Epstein tracked the group down to a small club, The Cavern, situated in a dank cellar in Mathew Street, Liverpool. The moment he saw and heard them he was smitten. Within weeks he'd become their manager and set them on the road to success. But the one thing they needed to break nationally, a recording contact, eluded them.

Despite Epstein's best attempts, every major record label in the country rejected The Beatles. But a series of lucky breaks led Epstein to George Martin, manager of Parlophone Records, who offered an audition at EMI Recording Studios, London, on June 6. He wasn't impressed, but on hearing "Love Me Do" offered the group a contract.

Two months after becoming EMI recording artists their drummer, Pete Best, was sacked. He was replaced by Richard Starkey a.k.a. Ringo Starr. The transformation was complete. By the end of 1963, The Beatles had four number 1 singles and two chart topping albums under their belts. Beatlemania was born and they'd become the greatest show business sensation the country had ever seen.

On February 7, 1964, The Beatles were greeted at Kennedy Airport, New York, by hundreds of screaming fans. They arrived with a number 1 single, "I Want To Hold Your Hand," a headline appearance on the *Ed Sullivan Show* – watched by an estimated 73 million people – and a string of sold out concerts. Beatlemania was now a global phenomenon.

By April 1964 The Beatles had 14 records in the *Billboard* Hot 100 with five of them holding the top five places. A film, *A Hard Day's Night*, followed, as did more sell out tours of Europe and America. Lennon also found time to publish his first book, *In His Own Write*, based on his schoolboy writings. A second book, *A Spaniard in the Works* was published the following year.

On August 15, 1965 The Beatles opened their third American tour in New York at Shea Stadium – the first time a stadium was used for a rock concert. 55,000 fans packed the venue and created a new world record for attendance and revenue generation. The tour followed the release of their second film, *Help!* If anything, 1965 was even more successful than the previous record-breaking year.

1966, however, was a turning point. A tour of the Far East ended on a sour note when the group was perceived to have "snubbed" Imelda Marcos. Things came to a head during The Beatles' fourth and last American tour. An off-hand remark by Lennon in the London *Evening Standard*, where he suggested that The Beatles were more popular than Jesus, was taken out of context by *Datebook* magazine, and resulted in the public burning of Beatles' records across America. The Beatles gave their last public performance at San Francisco's Candlestick Park on August 29, 1966.

For the first time in years, The Beatles had some time on their hands. Lennon headed for Spain and a part in Richard Lester's anti-war film, *How I Won The War*. Lennon's character wore round, steel-framed spectacles, which subsequently became his trademark. Although distanced from The Beatles, he continued to write for them and composed "Strawberry Fields Forever" while filming in Almeria. Destined for The Beatles' *Sgt Pepper's Lonely Hearts Club Band* album, it was issued as a single in February 1967.

In June, The Beatles performed Lennon's "All You Need Is Love" on the world's first satellite linked television program, *Our World*, to an audience of 400 million people. A search for something more lasting than material possessions led them to the spiritual teachings of Maharishi Mahesh Yogi. On August 25, they attended a weekend-long seminar in Bangor, Wales, with the Maharishi. Two days later Brian Epstein was found dead at his London home. It was the beginning of the end of The Beatles.

The Beatles' next venture, a film for television called *Magical Mystery Tour*, was a critical disaster. It wasn't the first time they'd experienced the critics' wrath, but it cut deep. In February 1968, The Beatles flew to India to continue their studies with the Maharishi. They left behind several projects including the production of their first feature-length animated film, *Yellow Submarine*, and the formation of their own company, Apple Corps. While in India they wrote enough songs to fill a double album, which they began recording on their return to England. The first song released from these sessions, "Hey Jude" – written by McCartney for Lennon's son, Julian – became their biggest selling single ever. A double album, *The Beatles*, was released in November and sold in millions. The following month, Lennon issued his debut solo album, *Two Virgins*, recorded with Yoko Ono.

By early 1969, The Beatles had reached breaking point. On January 2, 1969, they began filming what would become their last feature-length film, *Let It Be*. They were only days into filming when George Harrison quit the group. He was persuaded back, but the writing was on the wall. The group was racked by infighting, and on January 30 they gave their last public performance on the roof of their London headquarters in the heart of London's West End. But The Beatles weren't finished yet. In the summer of 1969 they regrouped at EMI Studios to record their swansong, *Abbey Road*. The *Let It Be* film and record limped on for another year and when it was issued in May 1970, it was described as "a cardboard tombstone," a sad end for the greatest pop group the world has ever seen.

60-61 Lennon photographed in Hamburg, Germany, with his friend, Stuart Sutcliffe, in the background. Looking every bit the rock 'n' roll hero, Lennon later said of his time in Germany, "I was raised in Liverpool, but I grew up in Hamburg."

62-63 Pete Best, George Harrison, John Lennon, Paul McCartney and Stuart Sutcliffe: The Beatles, photographed by Astrid Kirchherr during their first visit to Hamburg. They would return to Liverpool rock 'n' roll heroes.

64   Lennon photographed with Paul McCartney and Rory Storm backstage somewhere in Liverpool. The drummer with Storm's group The Hurricanes, Ringo Starr, would soon defect to The Beatles.

65   John Lennon with his '58 Rickenbacker 325 guitar. He bought the guitar in Germany in 1960. He later had it painted black and used it to record many of The Beatles early hits.

66-67 The Beatles with Pete Best on drums playing The Cavern Club in Liverpool. The Beatles played the Matthew Street club 292 times. It was where they were "discovered" by Brian Epstein, where they held the fan nights and where they first experienced early signs of Beatlemania.

68 and 69 The Star-Club was the largest of all the clubs The Beatles played in Hamburg. It was here that they were spotted by Bert Kaempfert and contracted to make a record with another Star-Club regular Tony Sheridan that would eventually lead to a management contract with Brian Epstein and a recording contract with EMI subsidiary Parlophone Records. 70-71 and 71 The Beatles prepare backstage for another concert somewhere in England. The collarless jackets they wore at the beginning of their career became as much a trademark as their mop top hair. Although the jackets were soon dispensed with, The Beatles hair, which was considered long at the time, influenced male fashion for years to come.

72 "I have never seen anything like it. Nor heard any noise to approximate the ceaseless, frantic, hysterical scream which met the Beatles when they took to the stage... No one could remain seated. Clutching each other, hurling jelly babies at the stage, beating their brows, the youth of Britain's second city (Birmingham) surrendered themselves totally," wrote Derek Taylor.

73 The Beatles' concerts could be riotous affairs. When they became a national phenomenon they were occasionally forced to cancel concerts because of security concerns.

74-75 While he was in Hamburg, Lennon co-wrote an instrumental, "Cry For A Shadow," with George Harrison. It would be the first and last time they shared a song writing credit.

1962

77 Lennon photographed in Hamburg by his friend Astrid Kirchherr. The Beatles early visual image was partly developed by Kirchherr, whose moody photographs became the benchmark against which all others were measured.

78 Astrid Kirchherr's iconic study of Lennon was so admired by The Beatles that they insisted Robert Freeman replicate the dramatic lighting effect for their second British long-playing record, *With The Beatles.*

1963

80 and 80-81 The Beatles take a well earned break and practice some new songs before a performance in Stockholm. The Beatles' tour schedule was so hectic that many of their early hits were written on buses or in hotel rooms.

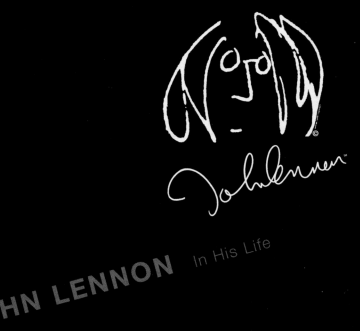

82-83 Ringo Starr and John Lennon enjoy a cup of coffee and a moment of tranquility at Stockholm airport before returning to the chaos that awaited them in Britain.

JOHN LENNON

84-85   George Harrison and John Lennon relax before The Beatles' appearance on the Swedish Television program Drop In. The Beatles performed their latest single "She Loves You," "Twist And Shout" and "I Saw Her Standing There."

1963

86 and 86-87 In November 1963, The Beatles performed at the Royal Variety Show at which Lennon made his famous remark, "The people in the cheaper seats clap your hands. And the rest of you, just rattle your jewelry."

1963

89 The Beatles perform their debut

1963

90-91 and 91 In December 1963, The Beatles presented their first Christmas Show at the Finsbury Astoria, London. During the 19 day run, The Beatles were seen, although probably not heard, by 100,000 fans.

1963

92 and 93   By the end of 1963, The Beatles really had something to shout about. They'd completed three British tours, a tour of Sweden, scored four hit singles, two N° 1 albums, appeared on countless radio and TV programs and won the hearts of thousands of fans. All that remained was America, and even greater success.

1964

94 and 95 Wherever The Beatles went they were greeted by hoards of screaming fans. In 1964 they arrived in Adelaide and were greeted by an estimated 350,000 fans, one of the biggest receptions they ever received.

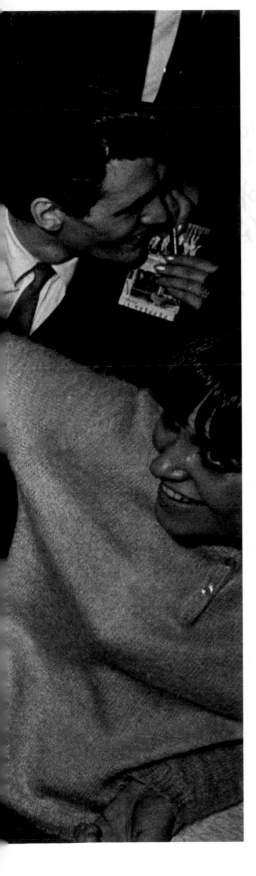

96-97, 97 and 98-99 Although pop stars weren't supposed to have wives or girlfriends, Lennon had obviously grown tired of pretending he wasn't married and took his wife, Cynthia, with him when The Beatles flew to New York for their appearance on the Ed Sullivan Show. As few people could afford to fly at the time, it would have been a big adventure for them, and they were obviously going to enjoy it.

100 and 101 When The Beatles arrived at New York's Kennedy Airport on February 7, 1964 they brought Beatlemania with them. Six days earlier they'd topped the U.S. charts with "I Want to Hold Your Hand." Their appearance on the Ed Sullivan Show was watched by an estimated 73 million television viewers, or about 40 percent of the American population. To say that The Beatles had arrived was an understatement.

103 Lennon poolside in Miami protects his trademark mop top haircut with a towel. In his right hand he holds another essential Beatles' fashion item, his pair of Chelsea boots, or as they were more commonly known, "Beatle boots."

104 and 104-105 Even though they were supposed to be relaxing, The Beatles were still called on to perform for the cameras. A photo shoot for Life magazine produced the classic photograph of The Beatles bobbing in a swimming pool.

1964

106, 106-107 and 108-109 From the cut of their hair to the cut of their smart suits and later hippie chic, The Beatles became the quintessence of Sixties' style, transforming the look and style of their generation and those that followed.

A hard day's night

111 and 112-113 Lennon and Mc-
Cartney take a break during the filming of *A Hard Day's Night*. While Mc-
Cartney works on another pop classic at the piano, Lennon contents
himself by reading a magazine. Directed by Richard Lester, *A Hard
Day's Night* represented a day in the
life of the Fab Four at the height of
Beatlemania; it was nominated for
two Oscars.

110

114 Lennon was the wittiest of The Beatles and could use the most mundane of objects to make light of often quite serious subjects. He could also be abrasive and often used his wit to destroy those he considered fools.

115 Lennon believed that the group he started was the best group in the world. It was a belief that sustained him and the other Beatles through the good times and the bad.

116 and 117 "I always was a rebel... but on the other hand, I wanted to be loved and accepted... and not just be a loudmouth, lunatic, poet, musician. But I cannot be what I am not." John Lennon.

118 *A Hard Day's Night* might have portrayed Lennon as carefree, but in reality he was deeply troubled. "The cocky rock and roll hero who knows all the answers was actually a terrified guy who didn't know how to cry," he said.

119 From the very beginning, Lennon and McCartney agreed to share credit on songs even if they were written individually. Together they would become one of the most successful song writing partnerships of the 20th century.

120 Besides co-writing 14 songs with McCartney for The Beatles' third British long playing record, *A Hard Day's Night,* Lennon also managed to publish his first book, *In His Own Write*, to considerable acclaim.

121 Because of his writing, Lennon became known as the "intelligent" Beatle. He published two books during his lifetime and co-wrote a stage play with Victor Spinetti that was based on his two books.

122-123   Lennon and actress Anna Quayle share a scene in *A Hard Day's Night*. Although Ringo Starr was praised for his acting, Lennon's performance was every bit as assured, and speaks volumes about his ability behind a persona.

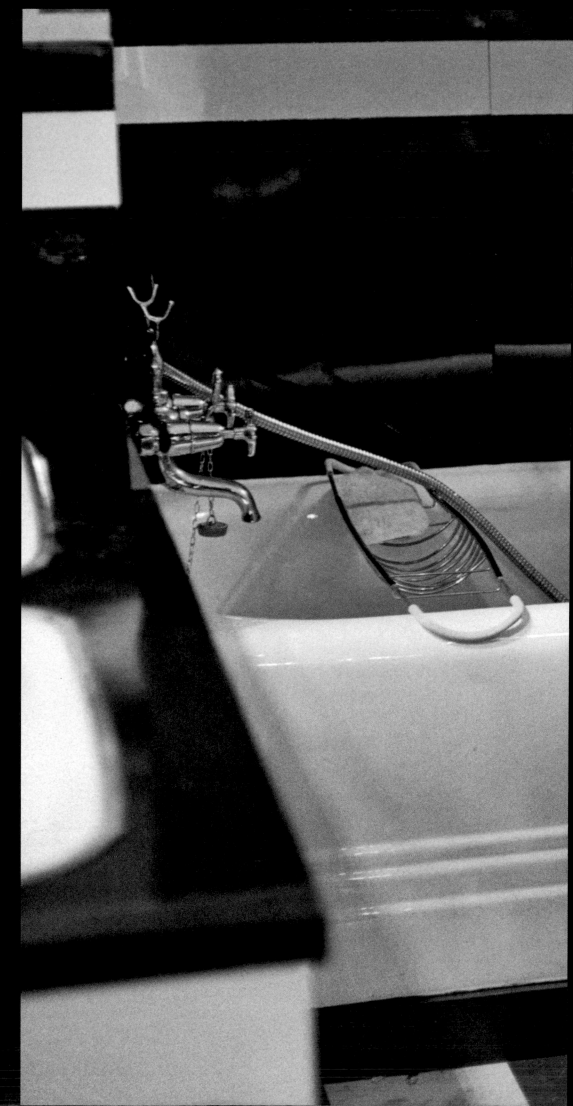

124-125   Lennon was still enjoying his fame, but he soon grew tired of the constant attention. "It [became] Beatles by numbers. Say something witty John, wear something wacky Paul. George you be strong and silent and Ringo – just be Ringo."

John Lennon

126-127 A classic shot of The Beatles from _A Hard Days Night_. Filmed on location in London, the biggest problem the crew faced was keeping one step ahead of the fans, who seemed to know instinctively where to find their heroes.

JOHN LENNON

128 Lennon had one of the best rock voices of his generation, but he was riddled with self-doubt and always insisted that The Beatles' producer George Martin treat it with effects and double-tracking. In concert, he was undeniably charismatic and the perfect irreverent foil to his respectful partner Paul McCartney.

130 and 131 Lennon loved the freedom that being a rock 'n' roll musician brought him. But he soon discovered that it had its limitations, including the endless round of press conferences and inane questions from dull journalists.

To Violet
my life's work.
with all my sincere
devotion and ...
God ... you
John (Lennon) x

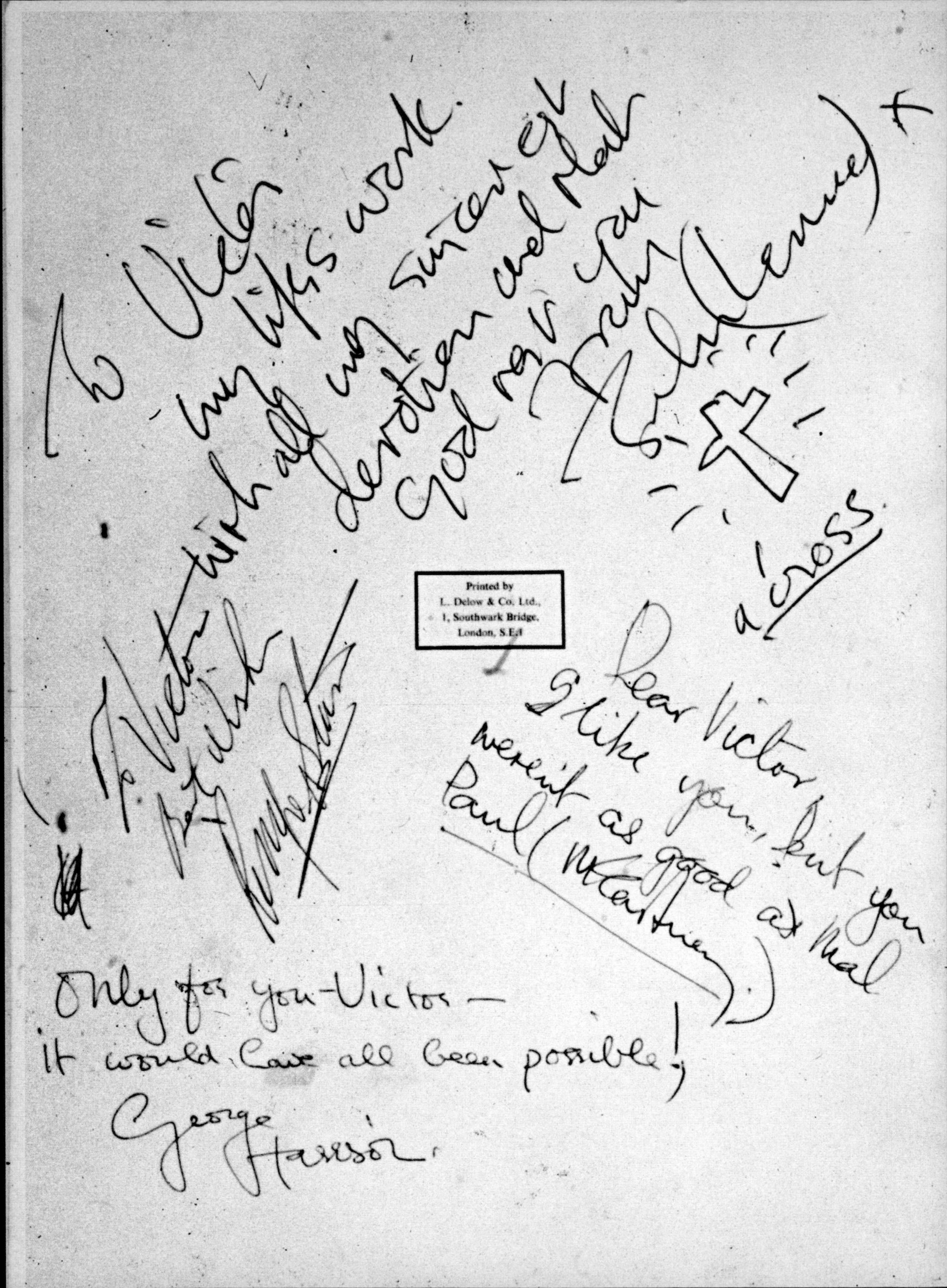

a cross.

Printed by
L. Delow & Co. Ltd.,
1, Southwark Bridge.
London, S.E.1

To Victor
best wishes
Ringo Starr

Dear Victor
I like your, but you
weren't as good as that
Paul (McCartney)

Only for you - Victor -
it would have all been possible!
George
Harrison

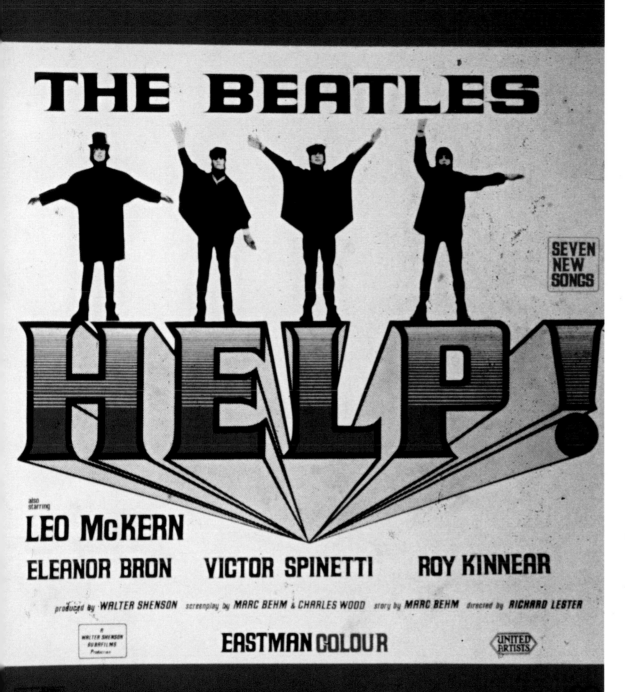

THE BEATLES

SEVEN
NEW
SONGS

HELP!

also starring

LEO McKERN

ELEANOR BRON   VICTOR SPINETTI   ROY KINNEAR

produced by WALTER SHENSON   screenplay by MARC BEHM & CHARLES WOOD   story by MARC BEHM   directed by RICHARD LESTER

A
WALTER SHENSON
SUBAFILMS
Production

EASTMAN COLOUR

UNITED
ARTISTS

ROYAL WORLD PREMIERE

THURSDAY 29th JULY 1965

LONDON PAVILION

PICCADILLY CIRCUS

132 and 133   The Beatles second feature-length film, *Help!,* also directed by Richard Lester, was another box office smash. Lennon, however, was less enamored with it suggesting that for most of the time they didn't know what was happening.

134 and 135   Ringo Starr and John Lennon on the set of The Beatles second feature-length film, *Help!.* Lennon was already beginning to grow disenchanted with The Beatles and would soon look around for solo projects.

JOHN LENNON

137 After two incredibly creative and arduous years, The Beatles could at last enjoy the fruits of their success. John took Cynthia to St. Moritz on a skiing holiday, but found it a little harder to master than the guitar.

138 and 139 By the time The Beatles came to make *Help!* their drug of choice was marijuana. The result was that for most of the time they were falling about like giggling school girls. "We were on pot then and all the best stuff is on the cutting room floor," said Lennon.

140-141 Lennon and Starr on the set of *Help!*. The pressures of being a Beatle were beginning to get to them. Lennon called it his "fat Elvis period" and Starr developed a nervous twitch whilst filming.

1966

142 and 143   Lennon pictured with British comedian Peter Cook in a scene from the BBC Television program *Not Only... But Also* in 1966. Lennon made his first appearance on the program in 1964 reading extracts from his book *In His Own Write*.

144 Lennon photographed in Paris on his way to Spain to begin work on *How I Won The War*. Two weeks earlier on August 29, 1966, The Beatles gave their last performance before a paying audience in San Francisco.

145 A year after filming his first solo acting part in Richard Lester's *How I Won The War,* Lennon was hard at work filming *Magical Mystery Tour* with the other Beatles. Here he is in Devon in September 1967.

1966

How I won the war

146 and 147 For his appearance in *How I Won The War*, Lennon played Musketeer Gripweed. His hair was cut short and he adopted round framed glasses for the role. This style of glasses became synonymous with him.

148 and 148-149 *How I Won The War* was Lennon's first significant anti-war statement and pointed the way to his later peace protests. While he was filming in Spain, he also wrote his psychedelic masterpiece, "Strawberry Fields Forever."

1966

150-151 Location filming for *How I Won The War* also took place in northern Germany. Unlike Spain it was cold and damp. With little to do between takes, Lennon soon got bored waiting to be called for his next scene.

152-153 Touring had become a physical and mental battleground that Lennon and The Beatles wanted to escape. The Beatles' world tour of 1966 was the straw that broke the camel's back. They would never tour again.

154-155 In June 1966, The Beatles played the Nippon Budokan Hall in Tokyo, Japan, to more controversy. Many in Japan considered the hall sacred and The Beatles' performances profane. To ensure their safety a reported 35,000 police officers were mobilized to protect them.

1966

1966

156 Prior to visiting Japan The Beatles returned to Germany for concerts in Munich, Essen and their old stamping ground Hamburg. Their patience with the media was already wearing thin and would be pushed to the limit as the tour progressed around the world.

157 Lennon would need to do more than pray when the tour arrived in America. A comment he'd made in an English newspaper about The Beatles being more popular than Jesus was printed out of context in an American teen magazine and uproar ensued.

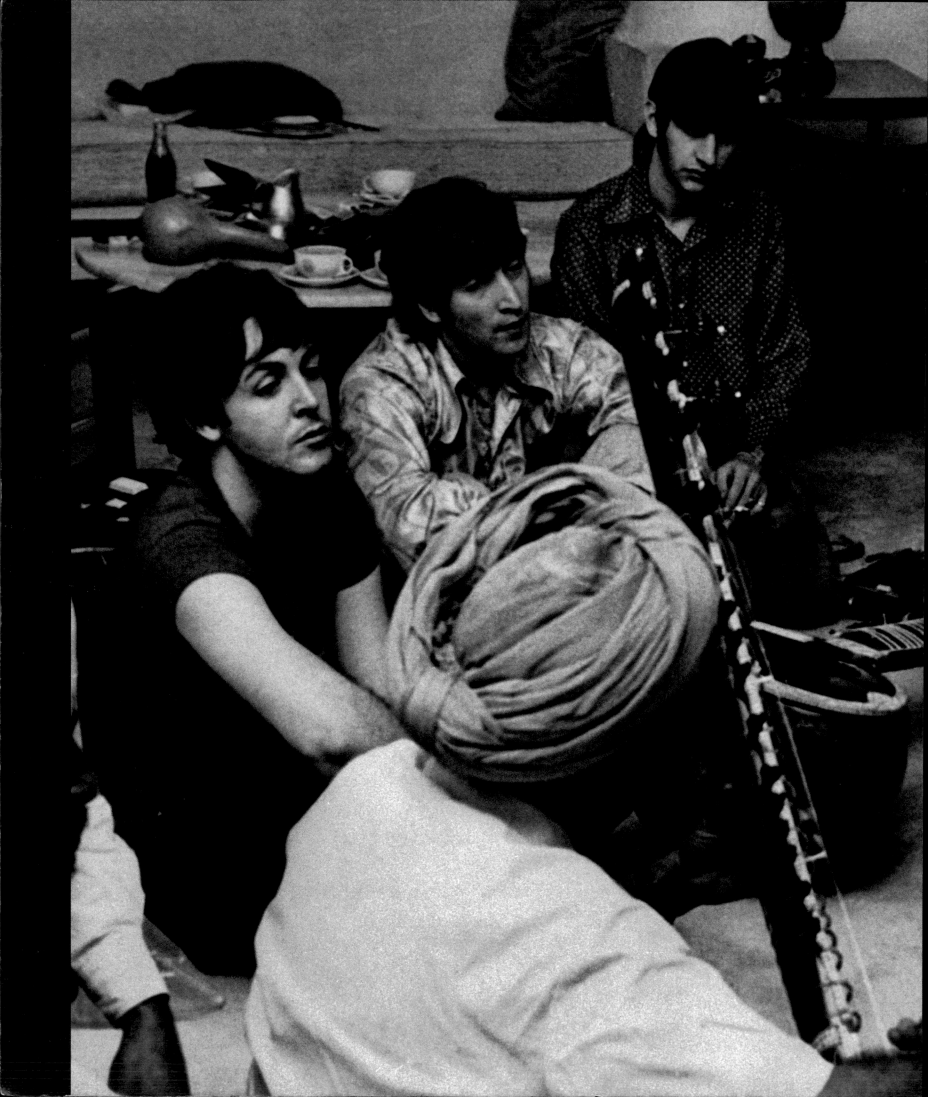

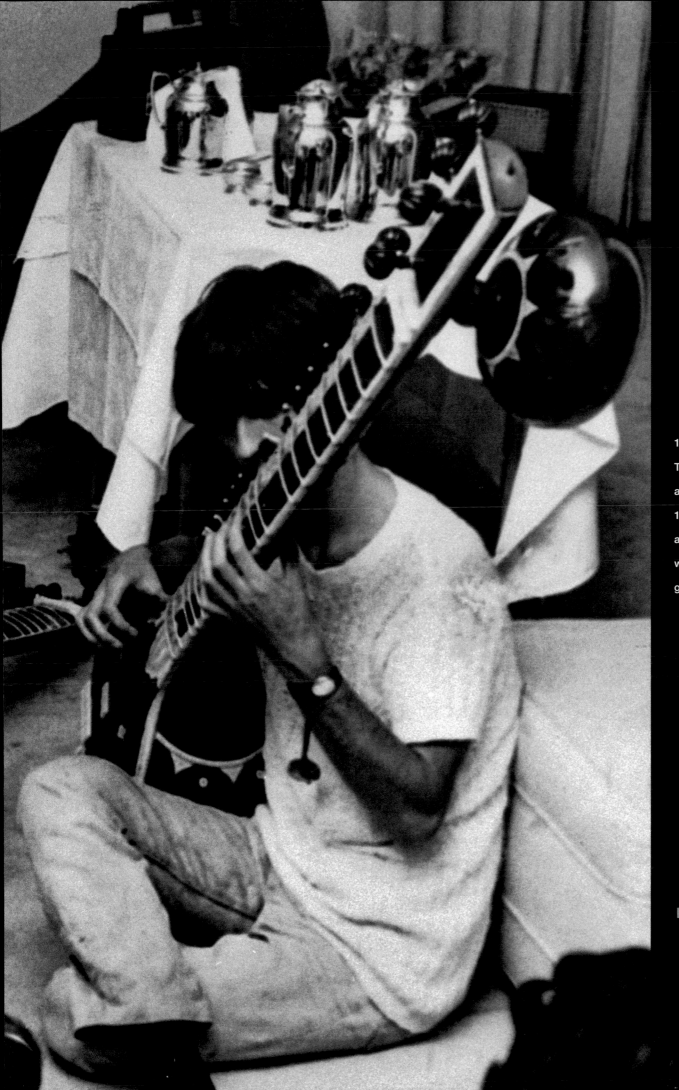

158-159 Thanks to George Harrison The Beatles developed an interest in all things associated with India. Their 1966 album, *Revolver*, featured Indian musicians, and soon The Beatles would look to Maharishi Mahesh Yogi for spiritual guidance.

1966

1967

160 The Beatles in EMI Studios, Abbey Road, London on June 25, 1967 with producer George Martin prepare to perform "All You Need Is Love" on *Our World*. The first ever global television link-up, *Our World* had a potential audience of 500 million.

There's nothing you can do that can't be done
and nothing you can sing that can't be sung
nothing you can say but you can learn how to
play the game —and it's easy.

There's nothing you can make that can't be made
no-one you can save that can't be saved
nothing you can do but you can learn to
be you in time — it's easy

There's nothing you can know that isn't known
+ nothing you can see that is in it's home
there's nowhere you can be that is not where
you're meant to be — it's easy.

161 Lennon's handwritten lyrics for
"All You Need Is Love." Along with
The Beatles' *Sgt. Pepper* album, it
became the soundtrack to the summer of love and was Lennon's first
song to promote peaceful change
through personal projection.

162-163 The Beatles do their bit to promote love, peace and understanding in a world ravaged by war and starvation. Lennon's anthem for love and peace topped the charts on both sides of the Atlantic.

1967

164-165 The Beatles remained incredibly busy throughout 1967. Besides recording their *Sgt. Pepper* album and "All You Need Is Love" single, they began work on a new McCartney-inspired film *Magical Mystery Tour*.

1967

Magical Mystery Tour

166 In July 1967, The Beatles went on holiday together to Greece. The group hired a boat to sail around the Greek islands with the idea that they might purchase one as a retreat from the mania they experienced at home. The idea came to nothing and rather than buy an island The Beatles poured their money into Apple Corps.

JOHN LENNON

169   On location somewhere in the west of England filming *Magical Mystery Tour*. The Beatles hired a bus and filled it with extras with the vague idea that a story would develop as they made their way across the country. It didn't.

1967

1967

170 and 171 Lennon photographed during a break in filming *Magical Mystery Tour*. Lennon's major contribution to the project was his psychedelic opus "I Am The Walrus," banned by the BBC because it contained the words "let your knickers down."

172 "We were all on this ship in the Sixties, our generation, a ship going to discover the new world. And The Beatles were in the crow's nest of that ship…" John Lennon

JOHN LENNON

174-175 The Beatles joke around for the cameras at the launch of their *Sgt. Pepper's Lonely Hearts Club Band* album. The album was, in part, a response to the Beach Boys' urbane Pet Sounds and helped usher in a new era of rock sophistication.

1969

177   Paul McCartney, Ringo Starr
and John Lennon rehearse their lines
for The Beatles brief cameo appearance in their animated feature-length
film, *Yellow Submarine.*

1970

178 and 179 The beginning of the
end for The Beatles, by this time they
were all but finished. Starr had
walked out of the group in late '68,
but was persuaded to return. Harrison did the same in early '69. By the
end of the year The Beatles would be
no more.

JOHN LENNON

180-181 On January 30, 1969 The Beatles gave their last public concert on the roof of their Savile Row headquarters in London. Although they were on the verge of breaking up, when it came to making music they could still find something to smile about.

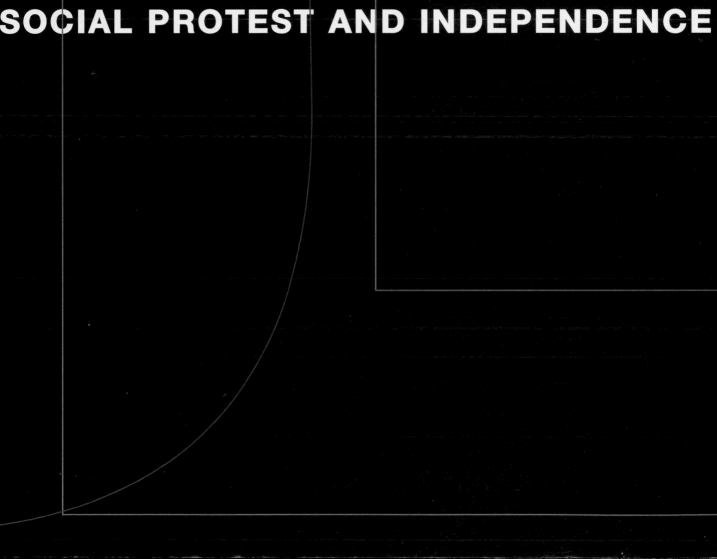

MEETING YOKO, SOCIAL PROTEST AND INDEPENDENCE

In the summer of 1966, John Lennon was looking for something, but he didn't know what. He found it in November that year when he met Yoko Ono at the Indica Gallery in London. Ono, seven years his senior, was born into a wealthy Tokyo family that encouraged her creativity – a rarity in Japanese society at the time. When her family moved to New York City, she enrolled at the Sarah Lawrence College to study piano and opera, before becoming involved with avant-garde art group, Fluxus. This eclectic group of artists and musicians made art that was intended to evoke a sense of continuous change.

Ono enjoyed socializing with artists, musicians and writers as they represented the freedom that until then she'd been denied. The Fluxus group of artists had a considerable effect on her, and later she encouraged Lennon to incorporate many of their ideas into his own songs and art.

Ono began creating works of art that were part poetry, part performance, part philosophical questioning. When she moved into her own apartment she turned it into an alternative art space, where she held "happenings" and avant-garde concerts. She became friends with the influential composer John Cage, and married her first husband, Toshi Ichiyanagi. They divorced in 1962, and in November that year Ono married Tony Cox, a musician and film maker, by whom she had a daughter, Kyoko. This marriage didn't last, but they didn't divorce until 1969.

In 1966, Ono moved to London to take part in the Destruction in Art Symposium, and later that year exhibited her "unfinished pieces" at the Indica Gallery – a bookshop and gallery. Invited to a private viewing by gallery owner John Dunbar, Lennon was immediately impressed with Ono's work, particularly her Ceiling Painting (Yes Painting).

Although they "connected" on their first meeting, it would be months before they got together. Soon after their first meeting, Ono began sending Lennon examples of her work in the form of postcards or "instruction pieces."

They intrigued Lennon, who soon became a patron and sponsor of her "Half Wind" show in October 1967. Lennon was hesitant at first and distanced himself from her world of black bags and Perspex boxes. He was still married to Cynthia and uncertain about his feelings for Yoko. Slowly, Lennon and Ono were becoming one. In May 1968, while his wife was on holiday, Lennon finally invited Ono to his house.

That evening they created a sound collage that became their first record, *Unfinished Music No. 1: Two Virgins*. In June, Ono began attending The Beatles' recording sessions and even sang on a record. Lennon and Ono became instant media celebrities. They were inseparable and were rarely, if ever, photographed apart. It became impossible to think of one without the other, to such an extent that they became "John andYoko."

Ono was the kind of intelligent and inspiring woman that was missing from Lennon's life. She became a surrogate mother and collaborator, encouraging him to look beyond song writing as his main creative outlet. Typically, he threw himself into the avant-garde art scene, something he'd previously dismissed. Ono's influence on his art and music was unmistakable. They considered everything they did to be art. Recording and filming constantly, they released four albums and the same number of avant-garde films in the space of a year.

Ono was a significant influence on Lennon's politics. 1968 was a year of riots in London, Paris and Washington. The Beatles had spoken out against the Vietnam War, racism and apartheid. The roots of Lennon's wish for social justice and global harmony were heard in his 1967 composition, "All You Need Is Love," but with Ono by his side he became considerably more vocal. Together they campaigned for peace, and did so with a series of witty Fluxus inspired events. Bed-ins, happenings and Bagism confused, angered and provoked a public still enamored with Lennon the acerbic moptop.

When the couple married in Gibraltar on March 20, 1969, they decided to use Lennon's celebrity status to send a positive message to the world. With the Vietnam War raging, John and Yoko began a multi-media campaign to promote world peace. They decided to spend their honeymoon in bed and invited the world's press to join them. On March 25 they moved into the Amsterdam Hilton Hotel and held their first "Bed-in for Peace." They gave hundreds of hours of interviews and explained their views on Vietnam and the peace process. The "Bed-in" was filmed and recorded, and formed part of the couple's aptly named *Wedding Album*.

The "Bed-in" generated acres of press coverage, but their actions were not universally acclaimed, and many found their form of protest frivolous. That didn't stop them from staging a second "Bed-in" at the Queen Elizabeth Hotel in Montreal in May. During the event Lennon found himself constantly repeating the phrase "give peace a chance." He turned it into a song, recorded it in his hotel room, and released it under the guise of the Plastic Ono Band. "Give Peace A Chance" quickly became the anthem of the anti-war movement and was sung at every peace protest.

Lennon's decision to release the single as The Plastic Ono Band wasn't simply a way of distancing himself from The Beatles; it was an act of solidarity with the people. The band was conceptual – anyone could be a member. John and Yoko wanted their audience to be involved in the creative process, which they believed would lead to positive social change. Their albums of "unfinished music," and the messages they sent out through their songs, were intended to encourage others to emulate and improve on their ideas.

"Instant Karma (We All Shine On)," written and recorded in one day, promoted the idea that people have the potential for greatness within them. But it also suggested that individuals should take responsibility for their actions and fate. In the months following its release, Lennon became increasingly involved in counterculture politics. He donated money to worthy causes, talked about radical politics and took part in public protests. In the autumn of 1970, Lennon recorded an album of intensely personal songs. *John Lennon/Plastic Ono Band* featured "Working Class Hero." A song intended for the workers, in it he argues for positive action, but he also acknowledges the personal limitations he faced in the struggle for social justice. The album closes with the statement that "the dream is over." His next album, *Imagine*, opened with a new dream.

It was Ono who inspired Lennon's best known song, "Imagine." Borrowing from her book, *Grapefruit*, first published in 1964, Lennon wrote an anthem for global humanism. He believed that people had the power to change the world. "Imagine" encouraged people to think for themselves, and consider themselves citizens of the world, rather than individuals defined by religion, possessions or nations. Like much of Ono's work, "Imagine" was an attempt to raise self-awareness and emphasize the act of self-creation. Lennon and Ono believed this could bring about a peaceful revolution that would benefit all mankind. Lennon's greatest statement, it offered a world of possibilities and was the culmination of his belief that personal projection could bring about positive social change. It became the song most associated with him.

The bulk of the *Imagine* album was recorded at Lennon's home in Ascot, England. It was finished in New York City, where, on August 31st, John and Yoko moved: to stay. No sooner had they arrived than social activist and co-founder of the Youth International Party (Yippies), Jerry Rubin made contact. Lennon loved the yippies' mix of radical politics and theatricality, and began planning an American tour to promote political activism.

Lennon was now at the height of his political engagement. He appeared at several benefit concerts, co-hosted The Mike Douglas Show – where he introduced Middle America to his radical friends – and recorded by far his most political album to date, *Some Time In New York City*. The album addressed such diverse subjects as Irish nationalism, racism and feminism – Lennon was the first and perhaps only male rock star to address this subject. His activism, however, brought him into conflict with the Nixon administration, which attempted to have him deported.

Lennon's fight to stay in America tempered his activism. He distanced himself from the radical left and political posturing. In a move that was typically thought provoking and irreverent, on April 1, 1973 he announced the formation of a new conceptual country, Nutopia. Its flag was a simple white rectangle, but it didn't mean he'd surrendered. His next album, *Mind Games*, took the ideas he'd posited with "Imagine" and added a deeper spiritual message. However, his quest for social justice had all but run its course. The records that followed were no less personal but a good deal less political. Although he became less overtly political, Lennon never abandoned his ideals. His last album, *Double Fantasy*, was inscribed with a simple message: "one world, one people."

With Ono by his side, his desire for universal harmony and social justice dominated his work. If he wasn't writing songs inspired by her art and ideas, he was writing songs inspired by her love. Songs dedicated to his wife are scattered across his albums. To the very end of his life he continued to be inspired by her. Their last album together, *Double Fantasy*, was intended as a dialogue in which they expressed their love for one another.

There can be little doubt that without Ono, Lennon wouldn't have undertaken the often unpopular and controversial protests he did. Neither would he have written some of his best loved and heartfelt songs. Ono left an indelible mark on Lennon and his work. She was indeed the "other half of the sky," that made Lennon complete.

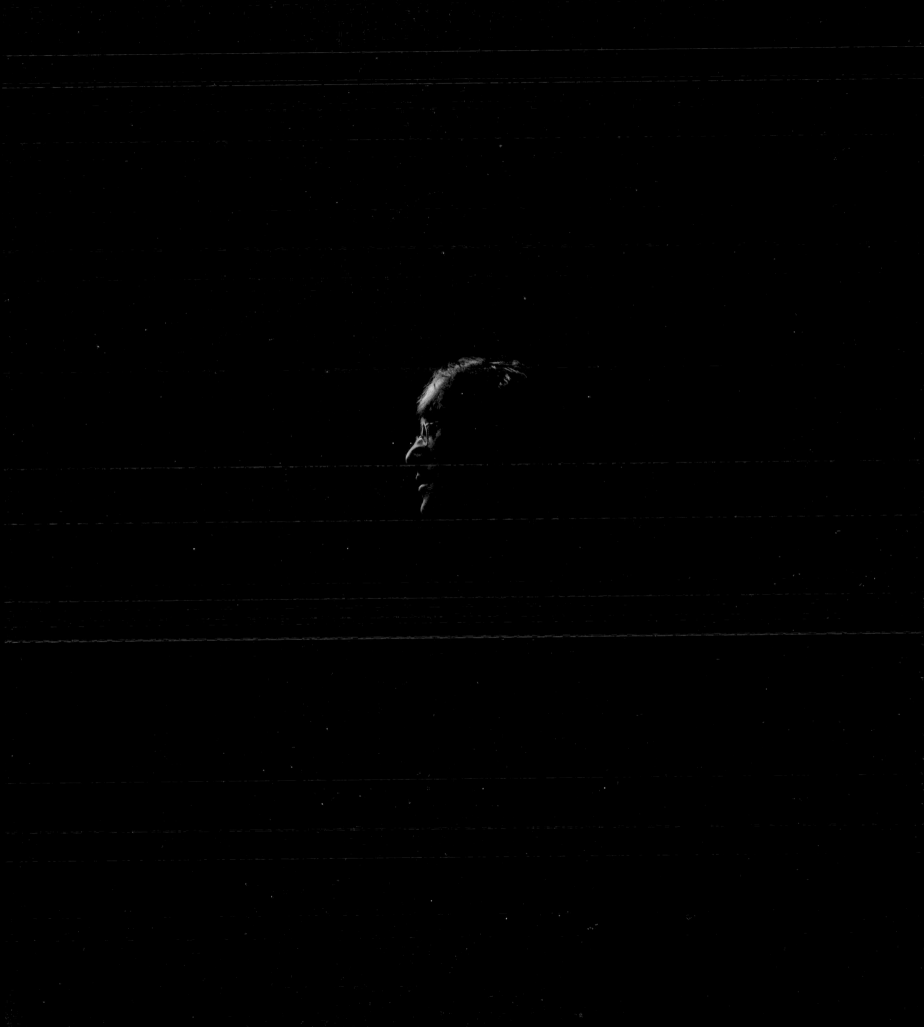

JOHN LENNON

184 and 193 "Before Yoko and I met, we were half a person. You know there's an old myth about people being half and the other half being in the sky, or in heaven or on the other side of the universe or a mirror image. But we are two halves, and together we're a whole." *Mr. John Ono Lennon MBE (Returned)*

194-195 John and Yoko were dreamers with visions of a more beautiful and peaceful world. Their ideas influenced an entire generation, and those that followed, to question conventional society and free themselves from it.

196 and 197 Besides attending The Beatles' recording sessions Ono sang on "The Continuing Story Of Bungalow Bill." She and Lennon recorded three albums of unfinished music together and a live album in the space of two years. They also shared "A" and "B" sides on several hit singles.

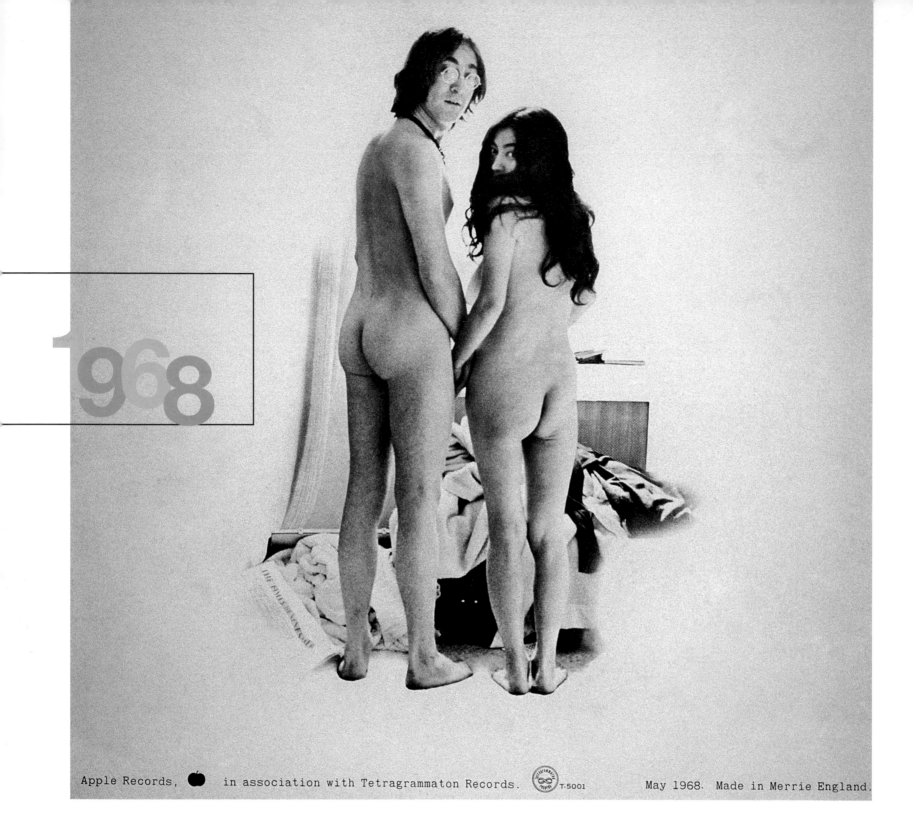

1968

Apple Records, 🍎 in association with Tetragrammaton Records. Ⓣ T-5001   May 1968. Made in Merrie England.

198 The back cover of John and Yoko's debut album. The front cover was a full frontal nude photograph of the cover that some found offensive. The Lennons considered it a work of art but even some of his band mates thought he'd gone too far.

199 Lennon and Ono issued their first album, *Two Virgins*, in Lennon's home studio at Kenwood in November 1968. An improvised avant-garde sound collage, it didn't sell well. The cover featured a photograph of the happy couple naked and created more controversy. John and Yoko saw it as a work of art, but the Establishment, particularly in America, had other ideas. Consequently, American copies of the album came with a brown paper wrapper.

Two Virgins.

200-201 Lennon said, "As usual, there is a great woman behind every idiot." Yoko was that great woman. He may have been inspired by other women in his life, but Yoko gave him the courage to break away from The Beatles and become a solo artist.

203, 204 and 205 In December 1968, John and Yoko appeared in The Rolling Stones' film *Rock 'n' Roll Circus*. The Stones' film was perhaps inspired by The Beatles' *Magical Mystery Tour* film. Lennon was filmed performing "Yer Blues" from the recently released *White Album*. Ono performed an improvisation with violinist Ivry Gitlis.

206-207 "We haven't been apart for more than one hour in two years. Everything we do is together, and that's what gives us our strength."
Mr. John Ono Lennon MBE (Returned)

208-209 Ono influenced many of Lennon's greatest songs, either directly or indirectly. Ono's instruction pieces were the main inspiration for "Imagine" and the couple also wrote several songs together, including "On My Love" and "Happy Xmas (War Is Over)."

1968

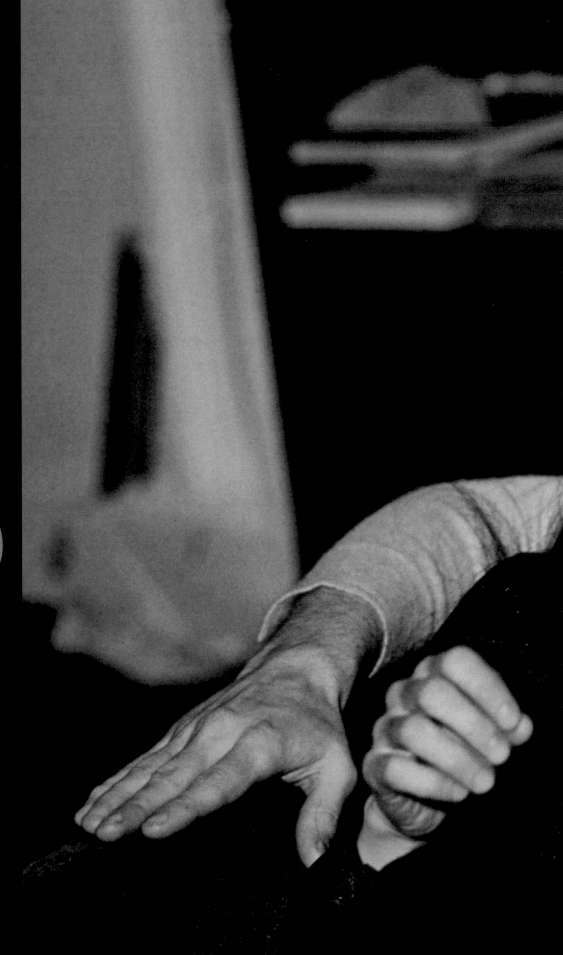

1969

210-211 John and Yoko championed the belief that personal projects on personal goals could bring about revolutionary peaceful change on a global scale. "The dream you dream alone is just a dream but the dream we dream together is reality," said Ono.

212-213 By 1969, John and Yoko had become inseparable. Together, they created works of art, composed music, made films, held exhibitions and embarked on a multi-media campaign to promote peace.

214   In 1969, Lennon spent more time promoting world peace than working with The Beatles. He was the first celebrity to use his fame to protest against the Vietnam War, and wrote the peace anthem, "Give Peace A Chance."

216 and 217 Lennon married Ono on March 20, 1969 in Gibraltar eight days after McCartney married Linda Eastman in London. Lennon celebrated the marriage and the events leading up to it by writing "The Ballad Of John And Yoko," the 17th and final UK number one single for The Beatles.

218 and 218-219 Six days after they were married in Gibraltar, John and Yoko moved into the Presidential Suite at Amsterdam's Hilton to promote world peace. The couple spent seven days in bed from where they gave interviews to the media and recorded part of their long playing record *Wedding Album.*

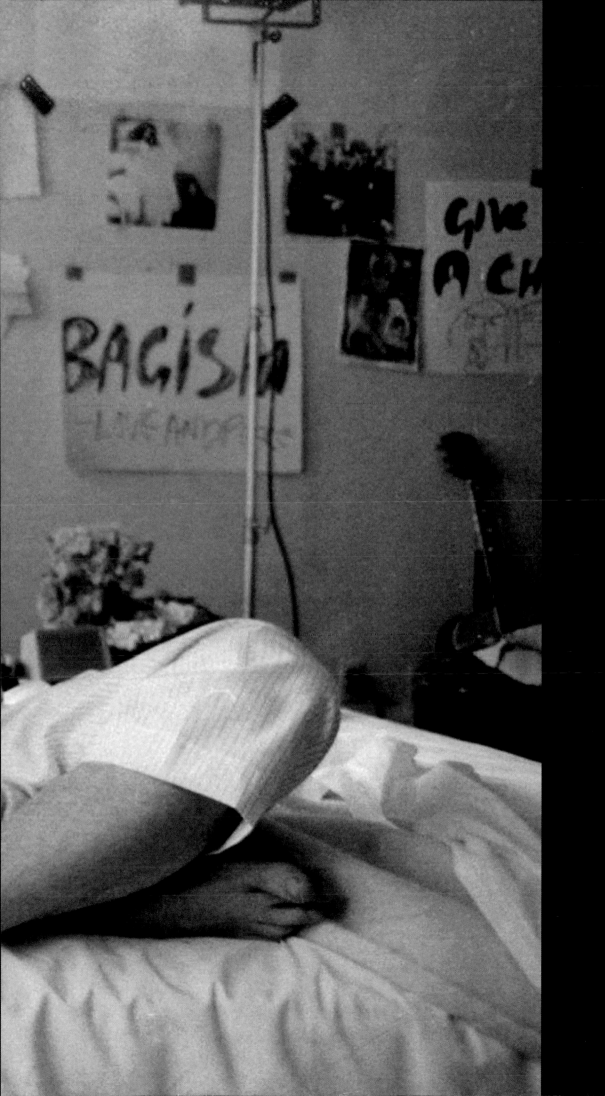

220-221 John and Yoko staged their second bed-in for peace at the Queen Elizabeth Hotel, Montreal, Canada, from May 26 to June 1, 1969. During the event, Lennon wrote and recorded "Give Peace A Chance."

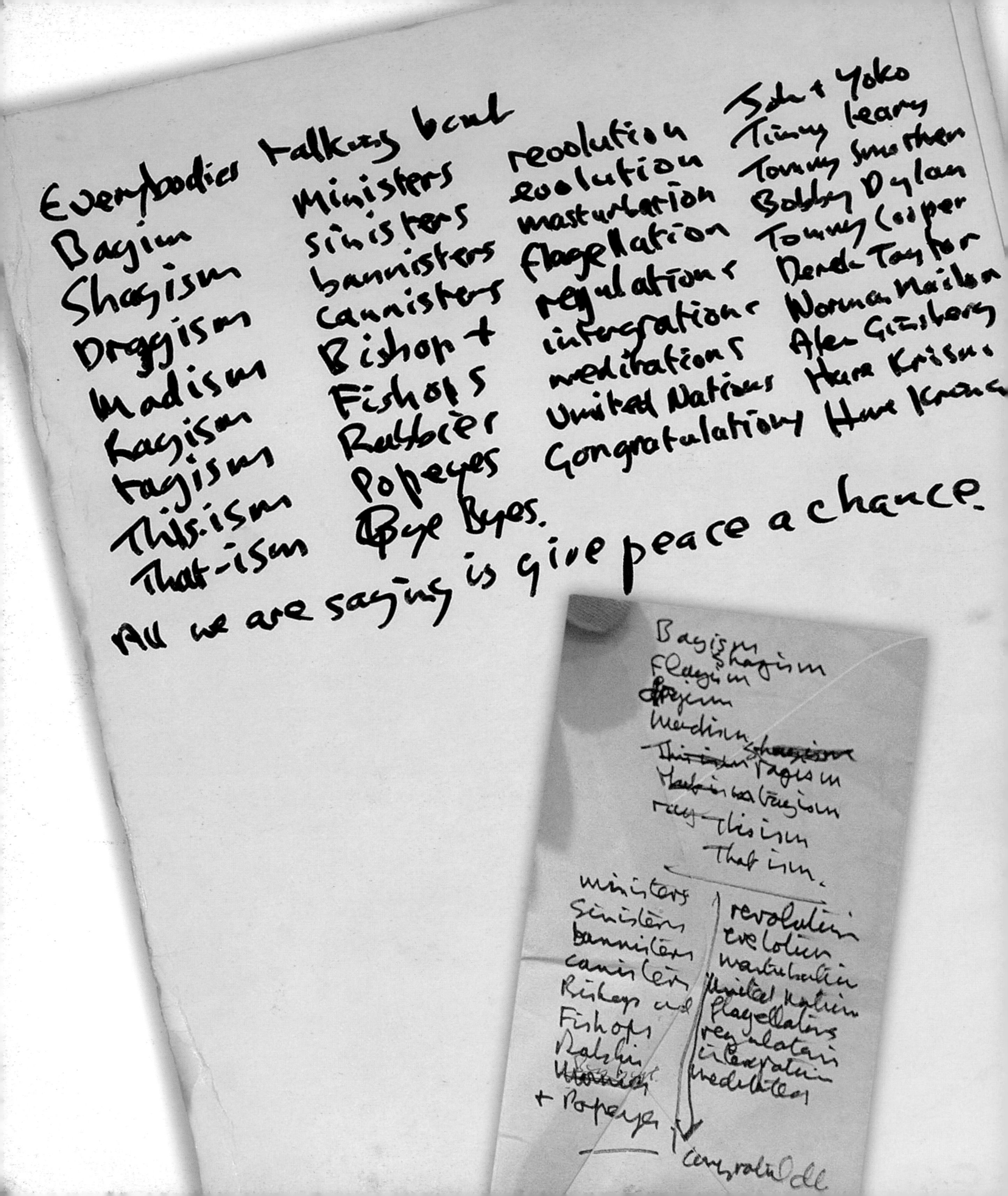

Everybodies talking bout

Bagism
Shagism
Draggism
Madism
Ragism
Tagism
This-ism
That-ism

Ministers
sinisters
bannisters
cannisters
Bishops +
Fishops
Rabbies
Popeyes
Bye Byes.

revolution
evolution
masturbation
flagellation
regulations
integrations
meditations
United Nations
Congratulations

John + Yoko
Timmy Leary
Tommy Smothers
Bobby Dylan
Tommy Cooper
Derek Taylor
Norman Mailer
Alen Ginsberg
Hare Krishna
Hare Krishna

All we are saying is give peace a chance.

Bagism
Shagism
Flagism
Dragism
Madism
~~This ism~~ ~~Shagism~~ Tagism
~~Madism~~ Ragism
~~Rag~~ This ism
That ism.

ministers
Sinisters
bannisters
cannisters
Bishops and
Fishops
Rabbis
~~Warmies~~
+ Popeyes

revolution
evolution
masturbation
United Nation
flagellations
regulations
integration
meditations

congratulations

All we are saying is give peace a chance

JOHN LENNON

226-227 In 1969, John and Yoko became living works of art. Everything they did, whether it was making music or staying in bed, became an artistic statement. Through their art, they made the private public in a brave move to show the world they were as vulnerable as everybody else.

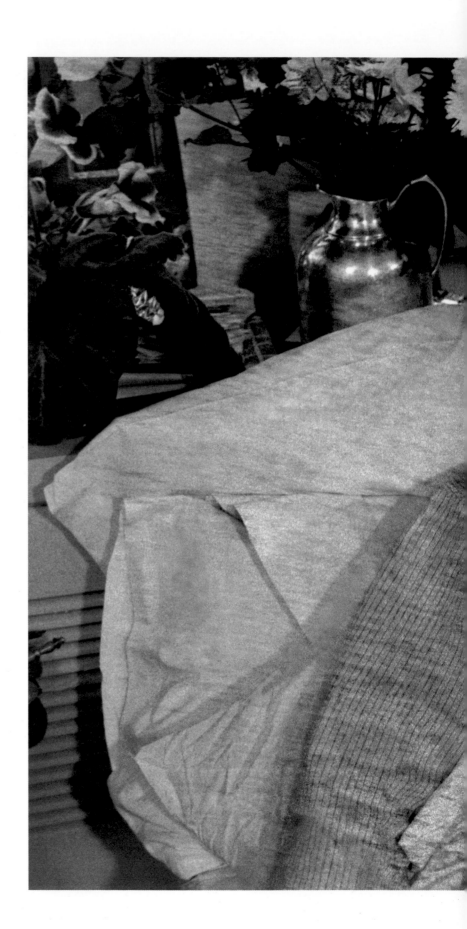

228-229 In April 1969, Lennon and Ono attended the Golden Rose of Montreux film festival where their film, *Rape*, had its premiere. The Lennons made several films together, all of them avant-garde or underground with limited distribution.

1969

230-231 In 1969, John and Yoko sent a "Package of Love And Peace" containing acorns and a personal message to world leaders. The acorns were intended as symbolic seeds of peace and of the East and West coming together.

1969

232 and 233 In 1969, John and Yoko developed one of Ono's earlier artistic creations into Bagism, a form of total communication. In April 1969, they appeared on a British chat show to explain the idea to a perplexed public.

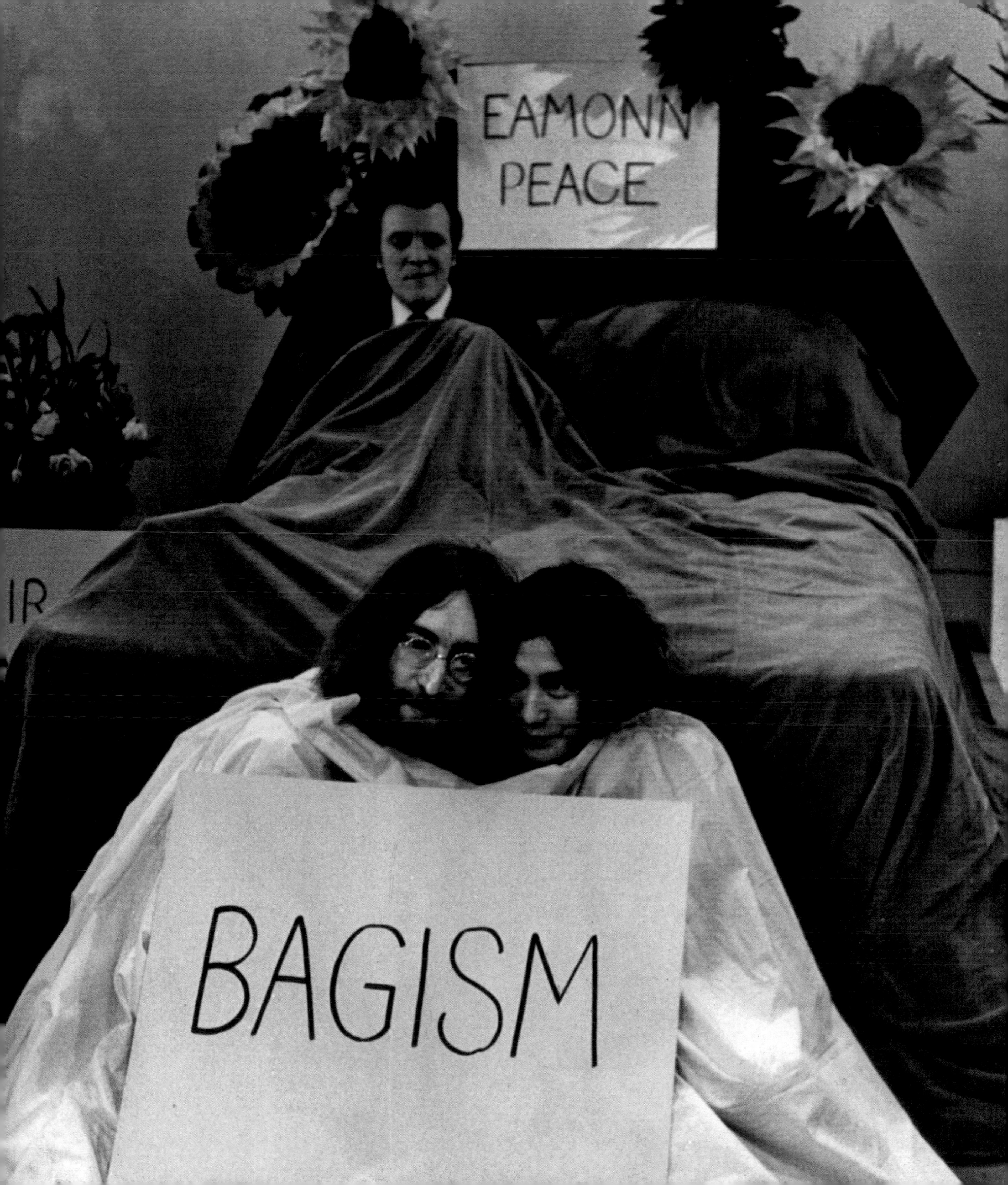
EAMONN
PEACE
BAGISM

JOHN LENNON

235 Kyoko, Ono's daughter by her second husband Tony Cox, with John and Yoko at Heathrow airport, London. Cox later disappeared taking Kyoko with him. The Lennons move to New York in 1971 was part of their attempt to obtain custody of Ono's daughter.

236 and 236-237 John and Yoko photographed at their office at The Beatles London headquarters. The Lennons used it as a base from where they gave interviews, promoted their records and concerts and championed the peace movement.

238 and 239 John and Yoko combined their artistic sensibilities to create their famous poster and billboard campaign "War is Over!" The posters were distributed to the world's major cities as part of a peace campaign protesting against the Vietnam War.

1970

240-241 and 241 John Lennon and Yoko Ono gave a bag of their hair to be auctioned to raise money for the Black House, in return for which they were given a pair of Muhammad Ali's boxing shorts.

1970

242 and 242-243 In February 1970, John and Yoko appeared in the British television program *Top of The Pops* to promote their single "Instant Karma (We All Shine On)." It was the only time Lennon appeared "live" on the show.

1971

244 and 245 John and Yoko moved
into Tittenhurst Park in Berkshire in
the summer of 1969. The Georgian
house, set in 72 acres of rolling
countryside, was the Lennons home
until late summer 1971 when they
moved to Manhattan.

246-247 Through their records, films, exhibition and concerts, John and Yoko showed the world that two ordinary people could make a positive difference. They were two creative geniuses who changed the world through the power of imagination.

248-249 Lennon was an avid reader of newspapers and would occasionally draw inspiration for his songs from them. *Red Mole,* which Lennon can be seen holding in his right hand, was a leftwing publication that published an interview with him in August 1971.

250-251 The *Imagine* album was recorded at Tittenhurst Park in the early summer of 1971. Lennon wanted to record the title song at the white piano in the large living room, but was forced to abandon the idea because of the room's poor acoustics.

1971

252-253 "When I fell in love with Yoko, I knew, my God, this is different from anything I've ever known. This is something other. This is more than a hit record, more than gold, more than everything. It is indescribable."

1972

254, 255 and 256-257 On August 30, 1972 the Lennons and Elephant's Memory played two benefit concerts at Madison Square Garden in New York in aid of the Willowbrook State School mental facility. They would be Lennon's last full-length concert appearances.

1972

258-259 and 259   By 1972 the
Lennons were resident in New York
and associating with radical left-
wing political activists. On February
5, 1972, John and Yoko joined pro-
testers calling for the withdrawal of
British troops from Northern Ireland.

1972

260-261 As the Vietnam War escalated, John and Yoko increased their political activities. In May 1972, the Lennons addressed 50,000 people at an anti-war rally in Manhattan's Bryant Park.

JOHN LENNON

263 John and Yoko face the press outside the U.S. Immigration offices in New York City. By now the U.S. government was fighting a losing battle. Lennon went on to win the case and remain in America for the rest of his life.

264 and 264-265 Although the Immigration and Naturalization Service deportation proceedings against Lennon were politically motivated, it argued that a conviction for cannabis possession made him ineligible for admission to the U.S..

267 After a trip to Bermuda, Lennon decided the time was right to re-enter the recording studio and record his comeback album, *Double Fantasy*, with Ono. It was the couple's first album to make number one on both sides of the Atlantic.

1980

PAGES 7, 8 MICHAEL OCHS ARCHIVE/GETTY IMAGES
PAGE 9 LEFT KEYSTONE/GETTY IMAGES
PAGE 9 BOTTOM ULLSTEIN BILD/ARCHIVI ALINARI, FIRENZE
PAGES 10-11 BETTMANN/CORBIS
PAGE 13 UNITED ARTISTS/THE KOBAL COLLECTION
PAGES 14-15 SUSAN WOOD/GETTY IMAGES
PAGE 19 UNITED ARCHIVES/PICTURE-ALLIENCE
PAGE 22 DAVID HURN/MAGNUM PHOTOS/CONTRASTO
PAGE 28-29 PICTORIAL PRESS/MARKA
PAGE 36 COURTESY OF MRS. YOKO ONO LENNON
PAGES 38-39 KEYSTONE-FRANCE/EYEDEA/CONTRASTO
PAGE 41 RUE DES ARCHIVES
PAGE 43 GEMS/REDFERNS
PAGE 45 M. HAYWOOD ARCHIVES/REDFERNS
PAGE 46 TOP, 46 BOTTOM, 46-47 COURTESY OF MRS. YOKO ONO LENNON
PAGE 48 TOP, 48 BOTTOM, 49 AP/LAPRESSE
PAGE 50 ULLSTEIN BILD/ARCHIVI ALINARI, FIRENZE
PAGE 51 MICHAEL OCHS ARCHIVE/GETTY IMAGES
PAGE 52 INTERFOTO/ARCHIVI ALINARI, FIRENZE
PAGE 54 JUERGEN VOLLMER/REDFERNS
PAGE 56 KEYSTONE/GETTY IMAGES
PAGE 60-61 STARSTOCK/PHOTOSHOT
PAGE 62-63 K&K ULF KRUGER OHG/REDFERNS
PAGE 64 ALBUM/CONTRASTO
PAGE 65 EVENING STANDARD/GETTY IMAGES
PAGES 66-67 TOPFOTO/ICPONLINE
PAGE 68, 69 K&K ULF KRUGER OHG/REDFERNS
PAGES 70-71, 71 PHILIP JONES GRIFFITHS/MAGNUM PHOTOS/CONTRASTO
PAGES 72, 73 BETTMANN/CORBIS
PAGES 74-75, 77, 78 K&K ULF KRUGER OHG/ REDFERNS
PAGE 80 FIONA ADAMS/REDFERNS
PAGES 80-81, 82-83, 84-85 POPPERFOTO/ GETTY IMAGES
PAGE 86 TOP RUE DES ARCHIVES
PAGE 86 BOTTOM CENTRAL PRESS/GETTY IMAGES
PAGES 86-87 GEORGE FRESTON/FOX PHOTOS/ GETTY IMAGES
PAGE 88 BETTMANN/CORBIS
PAGE 89 DAVID REDFERNS/REDFERNS
PAGES 90-91, 91 VAL WILMER/REDFERNS
PAGES 92, 93 FIONA ADAMS/REDFERNS
PAGES 94, 95 GAB ARCHIVES/REDFERNS

PAGES 96-97 BETTMANN/CORBIS
PAGE 97 POPPERFOTO/GETTY IMAGES
PAGES 98-99 UNITED ARCHIVES/PICTURE-ALLIENCE
PAGE 100 AP/LAPRESSE
PAGE 101 BETTMANN/CORBIS
PAGES 102, 103, 104 BOB GOMEL/TIME LIFE PICTURES/GETTY IMAGES
PAGES 104-105 JOHN LOENGARD/TIME LIFE PICTURES/GETTY IMAGES
PAGES 106, 106-107 EVENING STANDARD/HULTON ARCHIVE/GETTY IMAGES
PAGES 108-109 JOHN RODGERS/REDFERNS
PAGES 111, 112-113 MAX SCHELER/REDFERNS
PAGE 114 K&K ULF KRUGER OHG/REDFERNS
PAGE 115 MAX SCHELER/REDFERNS
PAGE 116 K&K ULF KRUGER OHG/REDFERNS
PAGE 117 MAX SCHELER/REDFERNS
PAGE 118 JOHN SPRINGER COLLECTION/CORBIS
PAGE 119 DAVID HURN/MAGNUM PHOTOS/CONTRASTO
PAGE 120 K&K ULF KRUGER OHG/REDFERNS
PAGE 121 DAVID HURN/MAGNUM PHOTOS/CONTRASTO
PAGES 122-123 UNITED ARCHIVES/ALBUM/ CONTRASTO
PAGES 124-125 DAVID HURN/MAGNUM PHOTOS/CONTRASTO
PAGES 126-127 BETTMANN/CORBIS
PAGES 128, 130, 131 MICHAEL OCHS ARCHIVE/GETTY IMAGES
PAGES 132-133 HULTON ARCHIVE/GETTY IMAGES
PAGES 134-135 STAN MEAGHER/EXPRESS/GETTY IMAGES
PAGE 137 TOPFOTO/ICPONLINE
PAGE 138 EXPRESS NEWSPAPERS/GETTY IMAGES
PAGE 139 EVERETT COLLECTION/CONTRASTO
PAGES 140-141 DPA/PICTURE-ALLIANCE
PAGE 142 TOPFOTO/ICPONLINE
PAGE 143 BETTMANN/CORBIS
PAGE 144 HULTON-DEUTSH COLLECTION/CORBIS
PAGES 145, 146 KEYSTONE/GETTY IMAGES
PAGE 147 JOHN SPRINGER COLLECTION/CORBIS
PAGE 148 EVERETT COLLECTION/CONTRASTO
PAGES 148-149 BETTMANN/CORBIS
PAGES 150-151 KEYSTONE-FRANCE/EYEDEA/ CONTRASTO
PAGES 152-153 HARRY BENSON/EXPRESS/ GETTY IMAGES

PAGES 154-155 BOB WHITAKER/HULTON ARCHIVE/ GETTY IMAGES
PAGES 156, 157 KEYSTONE FEATURES/GETTY IMAGES
PAGES 158-159 BETTMANN/CORBIS
PAGE 160 MICHAEL OCHS ARCHIVE/GETTY IMAGES
PAGE 161 CHRIS JACKSON/GETTY IMAGES
PAGES 162-163 BETTMANN/CORBIS
PAGES 164-165 KEYSTONE-FRANCE/EYEDEA/ CONTRASTO
PAGE 166 CENTRAL PRESS/HULTON ARCHIVE/ GETTY IMAGES
PAGE 169 HULTON-DEUTSH COLLECTION/CORBIS
PAGES 170, 171 DAVID REDFERNS/REDFERNS
PAGE 172 HULTON-DEUTSH COLLECTION/CORBIS
PAGES 174-175 JOHN DOWNING/EXPRESS/ GETTY IMAGES
PAGE 177 UNITED ARCHIVES/PICTURE-ALLIENCE
PAGE 178 EVERETT COLLECTION/CONTRASTO
PAGE 179 ALBUM/CONTRASTO
PAGES 180-181 EVERETT COLLECTION/CONTRASTO
PAGE 182 SUSAN WOOD/GETTY IMAGES
PAGE 184 BOB THOMAS/GETTY IMAGES
PAGE 190 TOPFOTO/STAR IMAGES/ICPONLINE
PAGE 191 AP/LAPRESSE
PAGES 193, 194-195 SUSAN WOOD/GETTY IMAGES
PAGE 196 EVERETT COLLECTION/CONTRASTO
PAGE 197 JOHN READER/TIME LIFE PICTURES/ GETTY IMAGES
PAGES 198, 199 BLANK ARCHIVES/GETTY IMAGES
PAGES 200-201 BOB THOMAS/GETTY IMAGES
PAGE 203, 204, 205 ANDREW MACLEAR/HULTON ARCHIVE/GETTY IMAGES
PAGES 206-207 TRAMONTO/AGEFOTOSTOCK/MARKA
PAGES 208-209, 210-211 TOM HANLEY/REDFERNS
PAGE 212 KEYSTONE FEATURES/GETTY IMAGES
PAGE 214 CHRIS WALTER/WIREIMAGE/GETTY IMAGES
PAGE 216 BOJAN BRECELJ/CORBIS SYGMA/CORBIS
PAGE 217 SIMPSON/EXPRESS/GETTY IMAGES
PAGE 218 BENTLEY ARCHIVE/POPPERFOTO/ GETTY IMAGES
PAGES 218-219 KEYSTONE- FRANCE/EYEDEA/CONTRASTO
PAGES 220-221 MARIO TAMA/GETTY IMAGES
PAGE 222 KEYSTONE FEATURES/GETTY IMAGES
PAGE 223 BETTMANN/CORBIS

PAGES 226-227 BETTMANN/CORBIS

PAGES 228 COURTESY OF MRS. YOKO ONO LENNON©

PAGES 228-229 BETTMANN/CORBIS

PAGES 230-231 POPPERFOTO/GETTY IMAGES

PAGE 232 BENTLEY ARCHIVE/POPPERFOTO/
  GETTY IMAGES

PAGE 233 BOB AYLOTT/GETTY IMAGES

PAGE 235 POPPERFOTO/GETTY IMAGES

PAGE 236 KEYSTONE-FRANCE/EYEDEA/CONTRASTO

PAGES 236-237 TOM HANLEY/REDFERNS

PAGE 238 FRANK BARRATT/GETTY IMAGES

PAGE 239 THREE LIONS/GETTY IMAGES

PAGES 240-241 BANDPHOTO/STARSTOCK/PHOTOSHOT

PAGE 241 TERRY DISNEY/EXPRESS/GETTY IMAGES

PAGES 242, 242-243 RON HOWARD/REDFERNS

PAGES 244, 245, 246-247, 248-249, 250-251
  TOM HANLEY/REDFERNS

PAGES 252-253 UNITED ARCHIVES/PICTURE-ALLIENCE

PAGE 254 BETTMANN/CORBIS

PAGE 255 AP/LAPRESSE

PAGES 256-257 BRIAN HAMILL/GETTY IMAGES

PAGES 258-259 AP/LAPRESSE

PAGE 259 JOHN RODGERS/REDFERNS

PAGES 260-261 BETTMANN/CORBIS

PAGES 263, 264, 264-265 AP/LAPRESSE

PAGE 267 BRENDA CHASE/NEWSMAKERS/GETTY
  IMAGES

Lennon Remembers: The Rolling Stone Interviews

By John Lennon, Jann Wenner

Published by Fawcett Popular Library, 1972

The Playboy Interviews with John Lennon and Yoko Ono

By John Lennon, Yoko Ono, David Sheff, G. Barry Golson

Published by New English Library, 1982

John Lennon: In His Own Words

By Ken Lawrence

Published by Andrews McMeel Publishing, 2005

The Lennon Tapes: John Lennon and Yoko Ono in Conversation with Andy Peebles, 6 December 1980.

By John Lennon, Yoko Ono and Andy Peebles

Published by British Broadcasting Corporation, 1981

John Winston Lennon

By Ray Coleman

Published by Sidgwick & Jackson, 1984

The John Lennon Encyclopedia

By Bill Harry

Published by Virgin, 2001

We All Shine on: The Stories Behind Every John Lennon Song 1970-1980

By Paul Du Noyer

Published by HarperPerennial, 1997

The Beatles anthology

By Beatles, Brian Roylance, Paul McCartney, John Lennon, George Harrison, Ringo Starr

Published by Chronicle Books, 2000

John Lennon: Listen to this Book

By John Blaney

Published by Paper Jukebox, 2005

The Longest Cocktail Party: An Insider's Diary of the Beatles, Their Million-dollar Apple Empire, and Its Wild Rise and Fall

By Richard DiLello

Published by Playboy Press Book, 1972

Beatles gear: all the Fab Four's instruments, from stage to studio

By Andy Babiuk, Tony Bacon

Published by Backbeat, 2001

The Beatles: A Diary

By Barry Miles, Chris Charlesworth

Published by Omnibus Press, 1998

Shout!: the Beatles in their generation

By Philip Norman

Published by Simon & Schuster, 2005

The Beatles: Off the Record

By Keith Badman

Published by Omnibus Press, 2003

Lennon Legend: An Illustrated Life of John Lennon

By James Henke

Published by Chronicle Books, 2003

Paul McCartney: many years from now

By Barry Miles

Published by Henry Holt and Co., 1998

Fab Four FAQ: Everything Left to Know about the Beatles-- and More!

By Stuart Shea, Robert Rodriguez

Published by Hal Leonard Corporation, 2007

WHITE STAR PUBLISHERS

WS White Star Publishers® is a registered trademark property of Edizioni White Star s.r.l.

© 2009 Edizioni White Star s.r.l.
Via Candido Sassone, 24 - 13100 Vercelli, Italy
www.whitestar.it

Editing: Jane Pamenter

ISBN 978-88-544-0449-6
2 3 4 5 6   14 13 12 11 10

Printed in Hong Kong

The Publisher wishes to thank Yoko Ono Lennon

for her helpful collaboration